INDIA: ACROSS AND AROUND

By

Prafull Goradia

Prints Publications Pvt Ltd

Published by

Prints Publications Pvt Ltd
Viraj Tower, 4259/3, Ansari Road,
Darya Ganj, New Delhi-110002
Tel. : +91-11-45355555
Fax: +91-11-23275542
E-mail : contact@printspublications.com
Website : www.printspublications.com

First Edition : 2023

ISBN 978-93-947910-6-0

Price: Rs. 595/-

Published and Printed by Mr. Pranav Gupta (Managing Director) on behalf of Prints Publications Pvt Ltd, New Delhi.

About the Author

Prafull Goradia, born in Bombay on 27th March 1937, is a specialist of the tea industry, having worked with the biggest tea-brokers in the world and later in his own business. He later made the conscious and resolute decision to quit a comfortable existence to enter the uncertain world of politics, his real passion and constant calling since his adolescence.

Elected to Parliament in 1998, as a member of the Bharatiya Janata Party (BJP), he intervened in several important matters that came up for discussion, making several significant speeches on contemporary issues, participating in debates and contributing to policy making.

Prafull Goradia has penned several books: Profiles of Tea, Dear Editor, The Saffron Book, Hindu Masjids, Muslim League's Unfinished Agenda, Anti-Hindus and Saga of Indian Tea, Fly me to the Moon (Bloomsbury India), Krishna Rajya (Bloomsbury India), Saffron Awakening, Had Patel been Prime Minister, Jinnah Helped Hindus, Population Exchange. He has also written over 500 articles on issues of both national and global significance. His letters to editors of national dailies, numbering over 2,800, are useful for transporting contemporary readers over a period of modern India's political journey. He presides over The Indian School in Delhi, which has earned a reputation for offering modern education entwined with traditional Indian ethos.

CONTENTS

1. ON BANGLADESH

Foreign Secretary Harsh Vardhan Shringla has in a public statement implied that Indo-Bangladesh relations are excellent. On the other hand, ISKCON has staged demonstrations at 150 temples across the globe in protest against the recent attacks on a temple as well as the murders of Hindus in Bangladesh. The demonstrations have been extended to outside private residences and other locations. A hundred and fifty countries have complained to the United Nations that Bangladesh should be asked to bring the lawlessness under control. The apparent contradiction is mysterious.

It is a pity that regardless of ideology, Bangladesh should treat Hindu temples and Hindus there in this manner. Have they forgotten that they would still have been slaves of their erstwhile western wing, but for the help and intervention by India's armed forces?

What East Bengal—now Bangladesh—meant to Qaid-e-Azam Jinnah is reflected in the fact that he had never visited it before March 1948. When he did visit, he addressed the Dhaka University only to tell its students that Urdu would be the sole national language of Pakistan, angering his audience.

Jinnah arrived in Dhaka on March 19th, 1948. On March 21st, he warned a large crowd at the Dhaka Race Course, against what he called the forces of subversion conspiracy bent on destroying Pakistan's unity. Feeble protests were heard from the crowd. Far louder voices of protest were to be heard only days later. The Qaid had through his Dhaka speech set East Bengal on a course that was to lead, over the next 24 years, to the break-up of Pakistan and the rise of East Bengal as the independent republic of Bangladesh.

Addressing a special convocation of Dhaka University at Curzon Hall on March 24th, an imperious Jinnah made it abundantly clear that "Urdu and Urdu alone" would be the language of the state of Pakistan.

Jinnah continued, "Our enemies, among whom, there are still some Muslims, have set about actively encouraging provincialism in the hope of weakening Pakistan and thereby facilitating the re-absorption of this province into the Indian Dominion. Those who are playing this game are living in a fool's paradise, but this does not prevent them from trying..." A sense of alienation between Jinnah and the Bengalis set in immediately with his departure for Karachi.

Evidently, Jinnah did not understand the psyche of the eastern wing. A Bengali, whether eastern or western, would rather give up his life than sacrifice his language. Overall, Bangladeshis can be estimated to be 65 percent Muslim and 35 percent Bengali in their outlook. For such people to be told that there is no Rabindranath Tagore or Qazi Nazrul Islam is nothing but sacrilege. Even today, the best Rabindra sangeet singer is Rezwana Choudhury Bannya, a Bangladeshi, who wears a sari and as well as a *tika* (mark on the forehead).

Regrettably, New Delhi's understanding of Bangladesh is not much deeper. There are a few liberals—quite a few—who still yearn for their lost Pakistan. The majority swing between "Sonar Bangla" and "Ab-e-Zamzam" in Mecca, the circumambulation of which is essential while on the Haj. The Bangladeshi media too oscillates between "Aakaash Paataal" and "Aasmaan Zameen". Another reason for the people of

Bangladesh being confused is that they never aspired for a specific nationhood after the British withdrawal. They could have been part of a united India, or a part of Pakistan, or of an independent Bengal, which Fazlur Rahman, Sir Abdul Rahim and Sarat Bose were negotiating during 1946-47. As it happened, they first landed with Pakistan and then became Bangladesh in 1971. For years therefore, the people of Bangladesh felt like nouveau-independent. If they are asked to make up their mind and choose, they are likely to go the Islamic way. The hateful Pakistanis are thousands of kilometres away, whereas the Hindu Bengali is only a border across. They are jealous of him because, for centuries, they served as his serfs.

Sheikh Mujibur Rahman had a career with the Muslim League for several years after 1947. If his daughter Sheikh Hasina Wajed were to be driven to choose, she would have no alternative but to go for Islam. That would be the choice of Bangladeshis, not necessarily for God, but for their identity.

Moving from culture to geography, to Bangladesh's east is Myanmar, with a well-equipped and capable military. On the west is West Bengal in India; the north again is India, whereas to the south is the Bay of Bengal, dominated by India. Therefore, conducting foreign policy from Dhaka is as difficult as anything can be. This is more so because the question is how useful can Bangladesh be to any big power. Its natural resources are limited. Traditionally, Bengal has been an agrarian area. Yes, the British did develop many industries, but only down the River Hooghly, notably jute, coal and iron. In other words, East Bengal did not obtain the benefit of development.

For its size, rising sea levels due to an increase in global warming is an awkward disadvantage. The options for Dhaka are few; be friendly with Myanmar as well as other countries like Nepal, and make sure that there is no slip-up in India's goodwill.

* * *

2. CRICKET AND PAKISTAN

It is disappointing that people living in India, enjoying their lives here support Pakistan celebrate its cricket team's victory over India. That shows such people are loyal to Pakistan and not to India. Pakistan is a country that broke away from India with the slogan "*Hans ke liya tha Pakistan, lad ke lenge Hindustan*".

Lakhs of Hindus were killed on their way from West Punjab to the east in 1947. Trains full of the corpses of slaughtered Indians would reach India to be received by their fellow countrymen. In this regard, an excerpt from Mohammad Ali Jinnah's speech of March 22th, 1940 at the Muslim League session at Lahore, a day before the League passed the Pakistan Resolution bears iteration.

"It is extremely difficult to appreciate why our Hindu friends fail to understand the real nature of Islam and Hinduism. They are not religions in the strict sense of the word, but are, in fact, different and distinct social orders. It is a dream that the Hindus and Muslims can ever evolve a common nationality. This notion of one Indian nation has gone far beyond its limits and is the cause of most of our troubles and will lead India to destruction if we fail to revise this misconception in time.

The Hindus and Muslims have different religious philosophies, social customs and literatures. They neither intermarry nor interdine, and indeed, belong to two different civilizations, which are based mainly on conflicting ideas and conceptions. Their views of life and of life are different. It is also quite clear that Hindus and Muslims derive their inspiration from different sources of history. They have different epics, different heroes in different episodes. Very often, the hero of one is a foe of the other and likewise, their victories and defeats overlap. To yoke two such nations under a single state, one a numerical minority and the other a majority, must lead to growing discontent and the final destruction of any such fabric that may be so built up for the government of such a state.

The termination of the British regime will be a worse disaster for the Muslims that has ever taken place during the last 1,000 years. Muslim India cannot accept any constitution which must necessarily result in a Hindu majority government. If Hindus and Muslims are brought together under a democratic system, forced upon the minorities, it can only mean Hindu Raj. Muslims are a nation according to any definition of a nation, and they must have their homelands, their territory and their state. We must be prepared to face all difficulties and make all the sacrifices that may be required of us to achieve the goal we have set in front of us."

Hardly had the flag of the newly independent India and Pakistan been unfurled when Jinnah sent Pakistani army irregulars called mujahideen into Kashmir. These terrorists managed to reach Srinagar airport before the Indian army reached the Valley, defeated and pushed them back.

The two countries have been enemies from their conception, not just birth. This is the country whose cricket team some of our citizens have cheered. Not merely a cricket win, but what is being advertised as a win for the religion of the country whose capital is Islamabad. It was no mere cricket celebration, but also a religious one, with the sole intent of insulting India.

The two countries have fought four wars in 1948, 1965, 1971 and 1999, to stamp the seal on their enmity. Each time, it was Pakistan that initiated the aggression while India defended itself. Even at present, there is a great deal of tension between the two countries. Terrorists keep sneaking into India literally every day. Nevertheless, if anyone loves Pakistan so dearly, he should shift to that country. They cannot enjoy Indian hospitality. Indians would feel relieved while Pakistan-lovers can enjoy life better in the country of their affections. Go, go, go is our request to them.

Now, let nobody compare this situation with Indians waving flags in England when the Indian cricket team wins in that country. It is simply not comparable. First, there is no enmity between India and Britain; there never has been. Yes, the East India Company chartered in London conquered India gradually. They took over Indian principalities but were never cruel. The Great Mutiny of 1857 then happened, leading to the Queen of England becoming the Queen of her Indian Empire. How the British modernized India is well known. They gave India as much as they took from it.

After we first requested and then agitated for them to leave, the British did leave peacefully and gracefully in 1947. They passed the Indian Independence Act and sailed to their home in an organized manner. There were no mass killings on the occasion of their parting. On the contrary, their Governor-General continued as ours. Earl Mountbatten remained the Governor-General of independent India for more than a year. There was beauty in such grace.

Not so with Pakistan. The fact that a mere T20 cricket match can bring out the worst jihadi impulses in that country only corroborates what their Qaid-e-Azam had bluntly stated in his Lahore Assembly speech more than 80 years ago.

Conversion

There were two reports on Sunday in national dailies relating to the much-debated issue of religious conversion. The first one is a statement by Dattatreya Hosabale, the General Secretary of the R.S.S. Hosabale has said that people changing their faith must disclose their conversion. The second report is about a lady Nisha who married a man who had not disclosed that he was a Muslim and married Nisha claiming to be a Hindu. She discovered his real identity well after their marriage. For some years, the husband has reportedly been pressuring her to convert and she was resisting. When the husband and could succeed, he along with his friends killed her.

Such confrontations of inter-faith marriages are being frequently reported. The phenomenon needs to be examined. One may refer to the Hadith when it is recorded that Prophet Muhammad exhorted his followers to shun celibacy and marry in order to produce as much progeny as possible. Marriage is enjoined upon every Muslim and celibacy has been frequently condemned by the Prophet. It is related to the stipulations in the Sunnah or Islamic traditions that Mohammed said, "When the servant of God marries, he perfects half his religion". On one occasion, the Prophet asked a man if he was married and being answered in the negative, asked him whether he was sound and healthy. Upon the man replying that he was, Mohammad replied, "Then thou art one of the brothers of the Devil" (*Mishkat-ul-Masabih*, Book XII). One of the Prophet's companions Usman Ibn Magun, wished to lead a life of celibacy but the Prophet forbade him.

Islam lays great stress on the numbers of its people. The same *Mishkatul* quotes the prophet "Marry women who will love their husband and be very prolific, for I wish you to be more numerous than any other people". Muslims are permitted to marry four free women and to have as many slaves for concubines, as they may have acquired (Qur'an; Surah IV 3). Mohammedan law fixes no particular age when discretion should be presumed (*Dictionary of Islam* by Thomas Patrick Hughes; published by Rupa & Co. Delhi).

Although the Quranic principle that there is "No compulsion in religion" (Qur'an Surah-II, Verse 256) is often quoted by those of the faith or those sympathetic to it to prove that the religion does not practice forced conversion, there can be no denying the historical fact that episodes of forced conversions have occurred in the history of Islam over the centuries. Neigbouring Pakistan, which was founded as a separate Muslim homeland and is a declared Islamic state, is particularly notorious for the abduction and forced conversion of Hindu, Sikh and Christian girls. This continues even today, in the supposedly modern 21st century.

The fountain of inspiration of the common Muslim, who indulges in such mischief as mentioned above, or "love jihad" for that matter, are his scriptures. This is the argument Mahatma Gandhi had used. When asked to comment on the Moplah riots of Kerala in 1921. He had said, "The Moplahs were following their religion. To that extent, they were not committing a crime". In 1927, one Abdul Rashid murdered Swami Shradhanand in the latter's sickbed. Gandhi, again, called the murderer "my brother". I suppose he was implying that both he and Abdul Rashid were religious individuals.

An Urdu teacher was associated with me for eight years, one afternoon in a pensive mood said to me that he was a "failed man". My surprised reaction was that he was a good and honest man. Why should he say so? Upon my probing further, he clarified that he was not a *badshah* (emperor) nor could become a rich man so that he could give employment to people. He was also no military commander who upon winning any battle, could convert people to the faith of Allah. He had not been able to marry owing to business failures, which could have enabled him to bring forth followers for his faith.

All these examples prove the innocence of the people, who marry wrongly because of deception. Even those who do so openly by declaring their religion are not necessarily immoral, but slaves of their faith. The reason why their want their wives who come from non-Muslim communities to be converted to their faith by the recital of the *kalima* (Muslim prayer of declaration of faith, enjoined as mandatory for every believer), is to make sure that their children grow up as Muslims and not half-caste. The fact that a greater number of such unfortunate girls are Hindu is because there are more Hindus. Hindus go to schools and colleges in greater numbers than Muslims and less conservative. Due to this easier contact, love jihad is easy.

Propaganda, rather than policing, is the suggested first step. The clergy should be contacted and told about the damaging communal consequences of these happenings, with also a request to pass on this message to as many young men as possible. Publicity through television and newspapers by the leaders of the community would be desirable. It is already becoming late and it would be traumatic for good young men and women to suffer damage or harm in any way.

* * *

3. DECEPTIVE RELIGIOUS CONVERSIONS

There were two reports on Sunday in national dailies relating to the much-debated issue of religious conversion. The first one is a statement by Dattatreya Hosabale, the General Secretary of the R.S.S. Hosabale has said that people changing their faith must disclose their conversion. The second report is about a lady Nisha who married a man who had not disclosed that he was a Muslim and married Nisha claiming to be a Hindu. She discovered his real identity well after their marriage. For some years, the husband has reportedly been pressuring her to convert and she was resisting. When the husband and could succeed, he along with his friends killed her.

Such confrontations of inter-faith marriages are being frequently reported. The phenomenon needs to be examined. One may refer to the Hadith when it is recorded that Prophet Muhammad exhorted his followers to shun celibacy and marry in order to produce as much progeny as possible. Marriage is enjoined upon every Muslim and celibacy has been frequently condemned by the Prophet. It is related to the stipulations in the Sunnah or Islamic traditions that Mohammed said, "When the servant of God marries, he perfects half his religion". On one occasion, the Prophet asked a man if he was married and being answered in the negative, asked him whether he was sound and healthy. Upon the man replying that he was, Mohammad replied, "Then thou art one of the brothers of the Devil" (*Mishkat-ul-Masabih,* Book XII). One of the Prophet's companions Usman Ibn Magun, wished to lead a life of celibacy but the Prophet forbade him.

Islam lays great stress on the numbers of its people. The same *Mishkatul* quotes the prophet "Marry women who will love their husband and be very prolific, for I wish you to be more numerous than any other people". Muslims are permitted to marry four free women and to have as many slaves for concubines, as they may have acquired (Qur'an; Surah IV 3). Mohammedan law fixes no particular age when discretion should be presumed (*Dictionary of Islam* by Thomas Patrick Hughes; published by Rupa & Co. Delhi).

Although the Quranic principle that there is "No compulsion in religion" (Qur'an Surah-II, Verse 256) is often quoted by those of the faith or those sympathetic to it to prove that the religion does not practice forced conversion, there can be no denying the historical fact that episodes of forced conversions have occurred in the history of Islam over the centuries. Neigbouring Pakistan, which was founded as a separate Muslim homeland and is a declared Islamic state, is particularly notorious for the abduction and forced conversion of Hindu, Sikh and Christian girls. This continues even today, in the supposedly modern 21st century.

The fountain of inspiration of the common Muslim, who indulges in such mischief as mentioned above, or "love jihad" for that matter, are his scriptures. This is the argument Mahatma Gandhi had used. When asked to comment on the Moplah riots of Kerala in 1921. He had said, "The Moplahs were following their religion. To that extent, they were not committing a crime". In 1927, one Abdul Rashid murdered Swami Shradhanand in the latter's sickbed. Gandhi, again, called the murderer "my brother." I suppose he was implying that both he and Abdul Rashid were religious individuals.

An Urdu teacher was associated with me for eight years, one afternoon in a pensive mood said to me that he was a "failed man". My surprised reaction was that he was a good and honest man. Why should he say so? Upon my probing further, he clarified that he was not a *badshah* (emperor) nor could become a rich man so that he could give employment to people. He was also no military commander who upon winning any battle, could convert people to the faith of Allah. He had not been able to marry owing to business failures, which could have enabled him to bring forth followers for his faith.

All these examples prove the innocence of the people, who marry wrongly because of deception. Even those who do so openly by declaring their religion are not necessarily immoral, but slaves of their faith. The reason why their want their wives who come from non-Muslim communities to be converted to their faith by the recital of the *kalima* (Muslim prayer of declaration of faith, enjoined as mandatory for every believer), is to make sure that their children grow up as Muslims and not half-caste. The fact that a greater number of such unfortunate girls are Hindu is because there are more Hindus. Hindus go to schools and colleges in greater numbers than Muslims and less conservative. Due to this easier contact, love jihad is easy.

Propaganda, rather than policing, is the suggested first step. The clergy should be contacted and told about the damaging communal consequences of these happenings, with also a request to pass on this message to as many young men as possible. Publicity through television and newspapers by the leaders of the community would be desirable. It is already becoming late and it would be traumatic for good young men and women to suffer damage or harm in any way.

* * *

4. INDIA v/s PAKISTAN

The recent war of words, law and politics began with Aryan Khan, the son of Bollywood star Shahrukh Khan, was arrested and kept behind bars for some weeks. Left-Liberals vociferously alleged that this happened because he is Muslim, forgetting that he is half Hindu. This controversy grew louder and worse when Indian bowler Mohammed Shami gave away a few runs to Pakistani batters in this T-20 World Cup. I feel this is a baseless allegation; and I am neither Liberal nor Left. To make matters worse, Pakistani Home Minister Sheikh Rasheed declared "Indian Muslims share our sentiment" which can mean that they are all Muslims first and then Indian or Pakistani later.

At Etawah in UP, the state's former CM Akhilesh Yadav has compared Pakistan's founder M. A. Jinnah to Nehru, Sardar Patel and even Gandhi. "They had all combined to win independence", said Akhilesh. UP CM Yogi Adityanath has taken strong objection to such comparisons, but no Muslim appears to have contradicted Akhilesh. There are innumerable such instances around the Muslim identity. The late Syed Shahabuddin repeatedly advocated the importance of Muslim identity above most issues. His pet expression was "Muslim Indian"; he refused to ever say "Indian Muslim". Clearly, he meant that the pan-Islamic loyalty supersedes national identity.

The recent example of the Pakistani winners of the recent T20 cricket match emphasizing that their triumph was that of

Islam, and not merely of Pakistan, is by no means an isolated one. Some years ago, when Wasim Akram was the captain of a Pakistani team that lost a match to Bangladesh, Akram said he did not mind as Pakistan had lost to a "Muslim brother". This clearly meant that the *ummah* is far higher than the nation.

This Islamic supra-nationalism is unpopular as was the Jewish sentiment of "Jew first, and German, British or French later." The origin of supra-nationalism is probably a Judaic phenomenon. Jews were captured by the Egyptians to work as labourers to build stone upon stone. It was clear that there was no Pharaoic intention to ever release them. The Jews felt cursed, miserable and hopeless. When their Prophet Moses, with Herculean difficulty, released them and led them to Israel, they could only think of God and overlooked any state or country. Ironically, they did not have either for centuries until the British helped them after World War II, in 1948.

Supra-nationalism has often been described as trans-nationalism, whereby a citizen's loyalty to his country is superseded by an allegiance beyond the borders to say, an empire, religion or something higher. In some ways, it is a suzerainty over and above sovereignty. A Jew's supreme allegiance is to Judaism and not to a country. Even after the nation called Israel was attained in 1948, for a Jew, Jehovah commands a higher loyalty. Chaim Weizmann, the leading figure in the movement for a establishing a separate homeland for the Jews and Israel's first president, illustrated the point by saying, "There are no British or French Jews; there are Jews in Britain and France".

It is telling that the acclaimed poet Mohammad Iqbal who wrote *Sare Jahan se Achha, Hindustan Hamara* came back from Europe, turned supra-nationalist and remained so. Yet he did not become a total separatist unlike Jinnah. In all probability, many a Muslim is similarly confused and is a prisoner of his feeling. Except the rich families, there is nowhere they can be welcome. Where then is there a place for supra-nationalist feelings? Have they, more particularly, not thought of what happened to the Jews in Germany and elsewhere?

The fourth Abrahamic sibling, Marxism too, is supranational in nature. Marxists, in adherence to their supranational nature and thinking, have destroyed their native countries. Does that mean that Muslims, who are also supranational, would end up by being destructive of their countries? Well, without the country of nature, their countries become poor. Their ethos does not encourage production or a productive culture. This has been explained most eloquently by Prof. Timur Kuran, who has proved how Islamic laws have held back the Muslim *ummah* in economic progress.

In sharp contrast, the Jews, who are also supra-national are believed to have the Midas touch. Their priority is the pursuit of wealth and successfully so. But Jews were unpopular in Europe, because they were suspected of caring more for themselves than for their countries.

The Marxists are another community of supranational without any faith in any god. In fact, they deny god and call religion "the opium of the masses". The objective of the communists is to unite the workers of the world. Their enemies were the rich or what they called the bourgeoisie, whose overthrow is necessary to what Marxists believe will be transfer of power to industrial workers or the proletariat. In a vicarious way, Marxists became enemies of even the small farmers by collectivizing or taking over their farms. In the end, the Marxist ruined entire countries, as their history proves it.

In the pursuit of its supranational ideology, Marxism also believes that the individual nation does not matter much. In fact, Marxism believes the nation-state to be an exploitative instrument of capitalists, just as Islam believes the nation-state to be the death of its faith.

* * *

5. LABOUR FREE MARKET

Every time wages and salaries of unskilled and semi-skilled workers are increased, by the government, my first reaction is one of gladness. The Government has raised their dearness allowance, effective 1 October. For long I have believed that teachers, especially at the school level, are the makers of the quality of our future society. As a consequence, the better the quality of society, the higher would be our civilization. The same logic does not apply to the wages of common workers in India at its present stage of economic development. The reason is if we raise wages statutorily, the employers, especially the small and medium businesses and industries would be scared away. They cannot all afford to pay more, most of the time.

Regardless, we must realize that industry or manufacturing is an employer of machines, not of men or women. True, it generates employment down the line in the shape of transport, of canteens, of dealers of shops and generally push the economy forward. But an efficient employer is in constant search of reducing the number of heads per machine. The intent is to control the unit cost of his product. The raw materials, packing, electricity are supplied by others who control their respective cost of production. But the man to machine ratio perhaps the employer is able to keep some control. The reality is that anyone who is skilled and can get a job at Rs. 20,000 would not work for Rs. 19,000. The government need not worry about his wages and welfare. The scheme of minimum wages that the government tries to ensure, if not enforce, is for those who are not easily employable; they do not have either the motivation or the skills to get a job on reasonable terms. By laying down a minimum, the government obstructs his prospects of getting a job.

The next thing that happens is a communal consensus among entrepreneurs that, it is safest to avoid labour intensive activities. For one, such enterprises are expensive, and worse, one cannot easily separate workers when the industry runs into a slum. On top of the statutory wages are the trade unions. What the unions can be, one would know if one has worked in Kolkata or in Kerala. In the latter state, even the class IV workers individually know what the law says. They do not need the union leaders to argue for them.

If, we prefer full employment, a change of policy is required. A lot of labour policy has come from the Industrial Disputes Act 1947, possibly the last legislation left behind by the British government before it left after Independence. An extreme left winger called Aneurin Bevan was in charge of Health and Labour. He gave Britain its national health service which is supposed to provide total health care to every citizen free of charge. Indians got the Industrial Disputes Act on which the entire labour ethos has grown. He did not realize that India was not Europe and we desperately needed employment and more employment as all under developed countries do. He visited Mumbai before he demitted office in 1952 and I have heard him speak for an hour at the Grant Medical College.

This legislation added to by the communist trade union attitude added up to an anti-employment formula for India. A job is better than none is our need. A person's skill and qualification will ensure him/her an adequate employment in any case. For the rest, there should be a free market. Between a person and a potential employer there should be freedom of negotiation of salary. So that the employee is not treated unfairly, there should preferably be a minimum monthly contract and a monthly notice of termination. With his salary packet, he/she should get a nationalized bank draft payable exactly five years hence for 25 percent of his wage. This would represent his savings like provident fund, gratuity etc. So that the employee is assured of his dues for his work life. The employer can terminate his services with one month's pay in lieu of notice. The salary would be free and depending on how much the employee is prepared to accept.

No other complication should come in the way of an appointment. With the size of our population and the and the number of young men and women coming on the market almost every day, this kind of a free market for labour is required. Remember, that agriculture would be freeing more and more workers who are likely to come to industry and service for jobs. At the rate we are progressing, anything like full employment would remain a pipe dream. If the licence to set up an enterprise is free, why control the wage level? That not only discourages employment but also creates an atmosphere of minimum employment.

An employee would expect an increment every year. Whereas a machine attracts depreciation which is a tax-free saving to the employer for eventually acquiring a replacement machine. This practice alone shows a preference for a machine over man from an employer's point of view. More need to be said to advocate wages that favour free appointment without any impediment.

* * *

6. GANDHI'S OFFER TO JINNAH OR GANDHI OFFERS PRIMEMINISTERSHIP TO JINNAH

What Akhilesh Singh of the Samajwadi Party and repeated by Rajbhar Singh of SBS Party about Mohammed Ali Jinnah being offered the first prime ministership of India to avoid Partition is incorrect. He was made the offer by Gandhiji although not supported by Jawaharlal Nehru and Sardar Patel or anyone else in the Congress. Jinnah did not even care to reply. He wanted a place in history's hall of fame which he could do best by founding a new country. According to his brother Ahmed, Mohammed Ali was obsessed with becoming the *numero uno*, nothing less or lower. Ahmed had said this to his friend and my grandfather Dharamdas Vora of 4, Girgram Road, Bombay 2 in 1946.

Holding a post can be a fleeting phenomenon as with any ministership while founding a nation is forever. In any case, the atmosphere amongst Muslims was so charged that they would have accused Jinnah selling out himself to the Hindus. And certainly not followed him into remaining in India. Also remember, Jinnah's health was generally known to be on its last legs; although everyone might not be aware of his suffering from tuberculosis of the lungs. Compare prime ministership for one or two years with being the founder of a nation for all time. Which would an intelligent person prefer? I would go to the extent of saying that Jinnah would not have enjoyed being the head of Pakistan for long. He delighted himself mixing with the elite whether Parsee, Hindu or Muslim. Rubbing shoulders with the common folk was not for him, who wore mostly Saville Row (London) hand tailored suits and English or Swiss shoes. His fancy for these items of attire was so great that he had himself buried in a suit and such shoes and not in pyjamas and a sherwani.

On his return from England to take over the Muslim League as President for life, he got down to building a magnificent bunglow which is still well known as Marble House on Malabar Hill, Bombay. As Claude Batley, its English architect told Hector Bolitho, Jinnah's first biographer, "He insisted on choosing the colours of the marble for the terrace, and standing by when the pieces of stone were fitted, much to the annoyance of the Italian stone masons doing the work." Besides the Italian stonemasons, Jinnah also hired a Muslim clerk of works, an English builder and a Hindu plumber."

People including the Muslim League members gossiped that, when Jinnah moved in 1940, that he was no longer Qaid but Qaid-e-Azam. That was how his admirer were impressed by the talk, if not also the sight, of the Marble House. It was rumoured to be worth Rs. 20 lakhs in 1941. Sri Prakasa, as Governor of Bombay came away impressed, he said, "I do not wonder that Mr. Jinnah's heart even as Governor General of Pakistan, was not in his Government House in Karachi, but in his house in Malabar Hill in Bombay."

Such a person could not fought for Pakistan with his heart in it. Remember until he returned from London in 1935, there were no politics in his life. And until 1928, he attended the plenary session at Calcutta and felt insulted, he had been a Congressman. So much so that Sarojini Naidu, the poetess politician had described Jinnah as the best ambassador of Hindu Muslim unity. His heart was in his law and its practice.

He was reputed to be the highest paid barrister in the British Empire. His head was for his name in history and the glory of it, certainly not being prime minister of India totally supported by Congressmen he did not trust. He often called Nehru 'Peter Pan' and Gandhi he did not trust. He had presided over a function in Bombay to welcome Gandhi when he finally returned to India in the year 1915. When Gandhi got up to reply he began by saying that he was so happy because he was welcomed by a *Mahomedan* leader. Jinnah publicly showed his irritation, if not also his anger, a reference to his religion for no rhyme or reason.

According to his brother Ahmed, they were culturally Parsee and not committed Musalmans or Muslims. They did not pray, did not know how to read namaz. They ate and drank what they liked. Mohammed Ali loved pork sandwiches and ate them openly. They enjoyed whiskey soda in the evening before dinner. His wife was Parsee named Ruttie until she died; his only child married a distinguished Parsee called Neville Wadia.

Campaigning for the 1945/46 general elections, he had stopped to make a speech at Jalandhar. Pran Chopra, who later became Editor of The Statesman, was then reporting on the election campaign. In the middle of the speech, reported Chopra, the azan was heard. So the crowd retired for namaz. Jinnah remained on the stage, sat down, put his hand in his *achkan* pocket and pulled out his cigar and smoked until the crowd returned and he resumed his speech in his eloquent English. How much the Jalandhar crowd understood, no one knows. Jinnah knew only English and Gujarati.

* * *

7. CHINA'S SETBACK, INDIA'S ADVANTAGE IN TAIWAN

It is in India's interest that China suffers a setback, ideally in East Asia, meaning on the Taiwan front. A particular reason is that the USA in recent weeks has repeatedly signaled its commitment to defend Taiwan's independence. The US Congress has passed laws that make it mandatory for the country to defend Taiwan in the eventuality of aggression by any other country, which in practical terms means China. India has no such guarantee and in an eventuality would have to fight alone, whereas for Taiwan's defence, Japan too would intervene.

It is true that in the early years, i.e., after Chiang Kai Shek's Nationalist Chinese Party lost China's civil war to Mao's Communists in 1949 and fled to Taiwan (then Formosa), the country made the mistake of calling itself the Republic of China and claimed the mainland as its continuation. In other words, Taiwan and China are the same country; in fact, the Nationalists of Chiang Kai Shek had declared Taipei in 1949 to be the capital of China which meant one country and not two. Until the 17th century, Taiwan was a base of operations for Chinese and Japanese pirates. The Portuguese were the first country to visit in 1590 and name it Ilha Formosa which means "Beautiful Island." During the 17th century, it was the Dutch and the Spaniards who settled on the island. The Taiwanese islands of Quemoy and the Pescadores Islands clearly point to European origins. They were however, expelled by a supporter of the Ming dynasty who had been defeated by the Manchus.

By 1842, Taiwan's population grew to 2.5 million. Thereafter, British trading companies too set up base in Taiwan, mainly to import tea.

Han China's Ming dynasty had annexed Taiwan in 1683, but had to cede it to Japan after the first Sino-Japanese war in 1894-95, in which Japan defeated China. The island was Japanized; while Japanese colonial rule was harsh, it economically developed and eventually industrialized the island country. Japanese became the language of Taiwan and remained its lingua franca until the end of World War II in 1945. The island was handed over to Nationalist China after Japan's defeat and surrender to the USA. However, after the Maoist victory in October 1949, Chiang Kai Shek and his Nationalists fled the mainland to take refuge in Taiwan. Chiang went on to become the head of state. During the Korean War in the early 1950s, the USA stationed its 7th fleet in the gulf between Taiwan and China. America soon began to give economic and military and to the island nation. In 1954, a treaty was signed which pledged the USA to defend Taiwan. China since the 1950s has adopted a militant posture towards Taiwan, claiming the island nation to be a breakaway province of the mainland, which has to be reunited, by force if necessary. In 1958, the Chinese fired artillery shells at Taiwan's coast. While this did nothing to win Taiwan, it certainly solidified American military support to the country. The USA sent more naval forces to protect Taiwan against any Chinese attempts at invading, and those naval forces have remained there since.

Geopolitically, the situation has remained more or less the same except that in 1971, Taiwan was made to yield its membership of the UN Security Council to mainland China. This was done as then US President Richard Nixon and his high-profile Secretary of State Dr. Henry Kissinger made their famous ice-breaking visit to Peking to call on Chairman Mao. The USA wanted to, and was successful in opening up China and completely weaning it away from the Soviet Union, which America wanted to contain and eventually defeat. This opening up to Communist China was a devastating setback for Taiwan. However, this was by no means an abandonment of Taiwan to the dragon. Economic, financial and social ties between the US and Taiwan continued to grow; Taiwan today is a developed country whose economy is one of the most prosperous in the world, and a leader in electronics, semiconductors and computer chips plus big industry. Also, the US defence treaty remained and still endures. With the embitterment in Sino-American relations over the last five years, Taiwan has come increasingly closer to the USA with increasing military aid flowing across the Pacific Ocean. Moreover, even in the years of bonhomie between Washington and Beijing, the USA never stopped selling advanced weaponry to Taiwan, which today boasts of a highly capable military.

Lately, Beijing has gone to the extent of accusing the USA of using Taiwan as a 'suicide bomber' against China. Experts have expressed fears of the situation of sliding into a full scale war between the two countries. There is no doubt that America has been training Taiwanese troops. Washington has raised the question of Taiwan's participation in the United Nations. The USA has the most advanced military while Japan has an efficient navy. Taiwan itself is now well organized and well armed. India has a quite a bit of territory to capture in Aksai Chin. Seeing all this gearing up, the Uighurs in Xinjiang and the Tibetans may be encouraged to rebel. Tackled by these five factors, Beijing may well see a change unwelcome to the current regime.

* * *

8. HINDUISM, HINDUDOM AND HINDUTVA

Anyone who believes in karma in the framework of his/her dharma is a Hindu. The dharma of a soldier varies from that of a pujari, that of a doctor is different from the dharma of a tailor. The dharma of a king or ruler is an onerous one compared to that of a shopkeeper. The former's integrity is all important for it would affect the whole country and all its people. To justify corruption by asking: which country in the world is free from corruption? The questioning prime minister claimed to be a Hindu and invariably wore a string of rudraksha. For a dominantly Hindu country, to tolerate such ignorance at the peak of its society is disgraceful.

The lack of full Hindu awareness could be attributed to the Abrahamic influence over our civilization. First, it was the Islamist invasions of Mahmud of Ghazni and then of Mohammed Ghori and so on. Next, much later, was the arrival, followed by conquest of the Christian East India Company. In between shipped in peacefully the Jews. Much later was the growth of Marxists who have had a substantial influence on Indian thinking especially the educated classes. Apart from politics, academics also influence thinking often much more.

The mix of Abrahamic and Hindu ideas on faith is a sad mismatch. The former four namely Judaism, Christianity, Islam and Marxism are scriptured on Deductive Logic where an assumed premise is given. For example, my god is so and so and he is the only god. Or there is no god; religion is the opium of the masses. Having prescribed such a premise, the

Deductive reasoning proceeds and it is virtually flawless in all cases because it is deduced from an assumed premise.

Hinduism has no such assumed premise. Karma is very similar to the reasoning in Physics where every action there is an equal and opposite reaction. Every karma has causes *bhagya* or fate, sooner or later. An illiterate peasant would, on enquiry, ascribe his poverty to his unfortunate karma in the past. He is unlikely to blame or curse the rich for having exploited him or his family. Which explains why Hindus are not a revolutionary people, but a tolerant culture and not easily excitable to violence. Despite the widespread poverty in 1947, communism did not get a country wide response while the Chinese went red faster than a river of blood. Beijing has only two close allies North Korea and Pakistan; it has annoyed the rest of the world. Can we ascribe this phenomenon to the paucity of faith or religion? Pakistan has pulled a curtain over its conscience due to its national poverty. Or else Islamabad would not be the running terrier of a civilization that is torturing and butchering brother Uighours in Xinjiang.

Hinduism is based on Inductive Logic which has no assumed premise; in fact, it has no premise at all. Its rise from the ground upwards, the reasoning moves up until a conclusion is arrived at. To illustrate briefly, supposing four Hindus happen to meet and discuss the flower rose. The northerner says roses are only red. The southerner asserts that they are only white. The Hindu from eastern India reports that he has seen only pink roses. On the other hand, the person from Maharashtra believes that the flower under discussion is yellow. There is likely to be a debate for say half an hour or more and the resolution might be that in each area the colour differs. Therefore, roses can have four colours depending on the soil; just because one has not seen does not mean that a colour does not exist. A staunch Abrahamic would adjudge that roses can be say only red; the rest are probably weeds or possibly breeds of other flowers, not roses. This is a sample of Inductive Logic in contrast to the Deductive approach.

As far as I know, the word Hindutva was first used by Rajnarain Bose, the grandfather of Sri Aurobindo in 1863. It only means Hinduness. I have recently written a book called The Grammar of Hindudom; rather like Christianity and Christiandom. There are no differences except of emphasis and context. Hindutva is used in the political sphere whereas Hindudom is written when dealing with the socio-economic-cum-political comprehensiveness. Remember, this is only ideology which has grown from the soil and under the sky of Asia. All others are alien. Marxism was written on a desk in the Library of the British Museum by a German in mid-19th century. Capitalism was formalized by Adam Smith in the 18th century. Fascism or class collaboration was conceived in Italy after World War I. Prof. Alfredo Rocco set forth the gist of the ideology leading to class collaboration in 1925 at Perugia. It was felt that capitalism had proved inadequate and unfair to the poor. Whereas communism was considered dysfunctional. Hence all the classes should combine to pull the society forward. The industrialists should be fair to their workers. If the latter felt dissatisfied, they should litigate but not go on strike. The young village men should get jobs as soldiers. To occupy them, when possible, the state should try to conquer territory abroad. An occasional war would generate demand.

* * *

9. WHY FEWER MUSLIM LEADERS?

Mr. Salman Khurshid's defence of what he said about Hindutva as well as others also defending him bring out a start fact. The Muslims of the sub-continent have failed to throw up a tall enough leader since Akbar, the Mughal emperor. Akbar showed the way of how to integrate with the rest of the populace. He conquered territory after territory, consolidated his empire and ruled for five decades. He made it possible for his successors to rule well for a century and poorly until 1762.

Thereafter, the British began to rule for nearly two centuries with a number Muslim starlets who had ideas but could not command the increasing followers. Sir Sayyid Ahmad Khan was a sincere officer who pleaded for educating Muslim youth but could not go beyond Aligarh and declaring that Hindus and Muslim were separate nations. Justice Ameer Ali was the first Indian High Court judge but migrated to England after he retired. Maulana Muhammad Ali was active and imaginative was obsessed with but retaining the Caliph on the Turkish throne was his uppermost priority and died early to have greater influence.

Poet Iqbal wrote an extremely popular song or *tarana*: *sare jahan se achcha Hindustan hamara* which even now Indian military bands play with alacrity. However, on return to India after a long tour of Europe, Iqbal underwent a revolution of mind and sponsored a division of India into the northeastern provinces and the rest. In short, he sponsored a confederate partition of India, he became a separatist.

Chaudhary Rehmat Ali, a Cambridge scholar, coined the name Pakistan and did little else. Thereafter followed Qaid-e-Azam Mohammed Ali Jinnah who was a true secularist until he arrived at the parting of ways with Gandhiji at the Calcutta plenum of the Congress in 1928. Earlier the popular Congress Sarojini Naidu described Jinnah as the best ambassador of Hindu-Muslim unity. He regularly wore lounge suits, never chudidar pyjamas and sherwani, suits which were mostly tailored at Saville Row London, the world's best for men's clothes. He became used to a peg or two of whiskey after sundown and enjoyed pork sandwiches in the afternoon. He did not know how to perform the namaz and seldom prayed any other way. This was so according to his brother Ahmed who was my grandfather's friend who resided at 401, Girgaum Road Bombay 2. According to him, they were culturally Parsee, Mohammad married a Parsee Ruttie Petit. Their daughter married Sir Neville Wadia.

Jinnah, in Gujarati is tiny, which was his grandfather's name. when he converted from the Lohana, a Hindu caste, he continued by being called Jinnahbhai but returned to India as Jinnah. He became a barrister in two years but was too young to be awarded the recognition. He had to stay back for two more years. He had learnt many an English habit and had no interest in religion.

On being side lined by Gandhi in the Congress, Jinnah went away to London to continue his law practice and became arguably the highest paid barrister across the British Empire. He had bought himself an impressive mansion in Hampstead in north London. In 1934, the Muslim League began persuading him to return to India because the party had become moribund. On the assurance that he would be President for life, Jinnah returned to Bombay. He dictated terms to the League whose other leaders did what Jinnah said. When the party did not do well in 1937 elections, he decided to blow the bungle for Pakistan on 22nd March 1940. To quote from his speech: The Hindus and Muslims have different religious philosophies, social customs and literatures. They neither intermarry nor interdine and, indeed, they belong to two different civilizations which are based mainly on conflicting ideas and conceptions. Their views on life and of life are different. It is also quite clear that Hindus and Muslims derive their inspiration from different sources of History. They have different epics, different heroes in different episodes. Very often the hero of one is a foe of the other and, likewise, their victories and defeats overlap.

The point we are stressing is that Muslims find it difficult to throw up a tall leader. Jinnah was successful in getting Pakistan but he played the role of a brilliant advocate rather than a leader. The only beneficiaries of Pakistan were a few migrants from UP, a few Gujarati businessmen from Bombay and the Punjabis who still dictate to the rest of their country centred around Lahore. The majority of Pakistanis went with Bangladesh. The rest feel that they are under the heal of Islamabad. Yet More Muslims remain in India than in Pakistan. Their economy is in a shambles it is still agrarian, if not also backward. The Khyber Pakhtunkhwa province and the hill districts are in the 19th, if not the 18th, century while Sindh is unhappy and Baluchistan wants to secede.

Incidentally, another beneficiary of Pakistan was Jinnah who established his place in the hall of history as the founder of a nation. What is the reason for the paucity of leadership? Is it the comprehensiveness of the scriptures? They have covered all aspects of life?

* * *

10. THANK SALMAN KHURSHID FOR EXPLAINING CONGRESS IDEOLOGY

Mr. Salman Khurshid has done a much needed service to the Congress by triggering of an ideological debate in the party. Until now, the popular impression was that the party was a platform on which politicians met for the pursuit of power. Ideas or ideologies were merely the responses to the challenges of the hour. When Gandhi felt that if Hindus and Muslims united, they could squeeze out the British by the early 1920s, he became president of the Khilafat Committee. This movement was to coerce the British to somehow retain the Sultan on the throne of Turkey. If they succeeded, he would also continue to remain the Caliph of all Sunni Islam. M.A. Jinnah stayed away from these gymnastics because he knew that final call would be taken by Kamal Pasha who was later called Atatürk and not by the British government.

When Gandhi saw that Turkish ice was not melting, in 1921, he gave a call for non-cooperation with the British Indian government. This involved non-violence which did not excite the Muslim saliva and they resorted to rioting; Malabar was a horrific holocaust of murder, rape and loot by the Moplas. When upbraided by Annie Besant, a past present of the Congress, Gandhi replied that the Mopla was obeying the rules of his religion. When the violent mood spread to Kohat in Baluchistan, Gandhi exhorted the Hindus to display their courage by allowing the rioters to kill them. He withdrew the Non-cooperation Movement because a police station was set on a fire at Chauri Chaura in UP. It was easier to retreat than to go on forward. In 1948, when K.M. Munshi came to Mani Bhawan in Bombay to seek Gandhi's blessing before any military action was ordered. The great man was silent on the subject of the action. Otherwise, his blessings were with Munshi.

In 1947, Nehru told General Lockhart, the interim C-in-C of the Indian Army, to wind down the force because we are a nation of peace and the police was adequate to protect India. Yet in 1948, we lifted tanks to the Kashmir Valley. In 1961, our troops were proud to conquer Goa, Daman and Diu, the Portuguese colony inside Indian territory. At Avadi in 1955, we swore by following a socialistic pattern of society while Nehru continued to reside in the British C-in-C's palatial bungalow at Teen Murti.

Indira Gandhi, at one stage, asked which country is free from corruption? She was generally right and stood absolved. She talked socialism and practiced the ideology as she understood it; she nationalized the Coal industry as well as 19 bigger banks and general insurance. No one explained to her that this was the adoption of state capitalism. Where was the society or the public in all this? Certainly nationalized assets gave the government power and patronage but the people generally remained poor. Gandhi and non-violence were overlooked so that we could march into East Bengal in 1971. It was a military victory but, at the same time, we removed a millstone around Islamabad's neck. We cannot deny that for the Congress, it was a military victory that ensured a landslide in the 1972 general election called 'Garib Hatao'.

Nehruvian socialism endured long enough until PV Narsimha had to overturn it overnight on coming to power in 1991. He had won the election on a socialist manifesto and governed with a capitalist goal. No one raised a question on the contradiction; ours is a considerate electorate. When the vigour provided by Rao's liberalization got exhausted, Indira Gandhi's grandson declared that the Congress was a Muslim party. Secularism was rubbed off the Congress blackboard with the ease of a soft duster.

Of all leaders, a BJP heavy weight once asserted at Bangaru Laxman's abhishek in Nagpur that governance is more important than ideology. Yes, this is partly true; because Narsimha Rao would have been chain bound to not liberalize in 1991 and India would have been in big economic trouble. On the other hand, ideology helps to bind party members together; whereas power can at best keep ministers together. That is one of the main trouble spots of the Congress today. This party depended on their top leader to hold them together; first M.K. Gandhi, then Jawaharlal Nehru, Indira Gandhi and Rajiv, even Sonia Gandhi. Once the leader is deficient in charisma, the problem begins. It is not that the current younger leaders are very weak but they are up against an unprecedented giant and his party. This has never happened never before. The Communist parties had the benefit ideology but it was a philosophy which had been washed away by history and its Soviet leadership was blissfully unaware.

Even Karl Marx was not aware of the lacuna in his theory. He was so obsessed with distribution that he overlooked the importance of production. He wanted the bourgeoisie out because of its wealth. But what about its managerial function; the party apparatchik is no replacement nor for that matter, the union leader. Being a theoretician, he could overlook but what was his friend and partner Friedrich Engels doing? Why did not Marx check with him?

* * *

11. UNIFORM CIVIL CODE

Some of the laws regarding marriage in India violate Articles 14 and 15 of the Constitution of India, which insist on the equality of all citizens. For a glaring example, a Muslim man is allowed to have four wives at a time, while a woman has to restrict herself to only one husband. The husband can terminate his marriage within three months under the *talaq* rules, but the wife does not enjoy this privilege of *talaq*. She must take the help of *khul*. Her release is possible only upon payment of compensation to her husband, which may or may not entice him to make him return the *mehr* or the dower, which was supposed to have been paid by him to her. In the event, the husband is not tempted by her offer of compensation, she would have to suffer a lengthy procedure before a council of *qazis*.

Evidently, these rules are not only unequal and discriminatory, but also misogynous, reflecting extreme bias and one might add, hatred of women, besides their being also anti-secular; no one other than a Muslim is allowed this privilege of so many wives with the privilege of a quick divorce. This is not withstanding Article 44, a Directive Principle of State Policy, enjoining upon the government the implementation of a Uniform Civil Code for all citizens of the country. When in 1955, the Parliament passed the Hindu Code Bill, Prime Minister Jawaharlal Nehru was asked by a Member of Parliament why nothing was being done on the question of a Uniform Civil Code. Nehru's reply to the member was: "Well, I should like a civil code, which applies to everybody, but wisdom hinders. If he (the member) or anybody else brings forward a civil code, it will have my extreme sympathies. But I confess that I do not think that at the present moment the time is ripe in India for me to try and push it through. I want to prepare the ground for it".

My anxiety is that these violations and contradictions leave the door wide open for our law courts to discriminate between communities in the domain of law. As for instance, whether wearing a *hijab* in school or college or such additional clothing is appropriate or even essential for some students, but not for others. If good for some, on grounds of either religion or freedom, why cannot another set of students come to classes with swimming suits or bikinis, on grounds of freedom and easy accessibility to the school's swimming pool?

That must naturally bring us to the attention of where does society, state and law draw the line as far as competitive religiosity of the mind that is now seen on an increased scale? More importantly, what does this mean for an avowedly secular state, whose constitution, at least on paper, forbids discrimination on the grounds of religion, caste, gender, race, place of birth, etc. In this entire context, we cannot avoid the crucial question of a Uniform Civil Code, which is among other things, polygamy, is enough to render the country's claim to be a secular democracy a meaningless one.

Laws especially in a secular democracy, have to be equal for all its citizens. No religious law can be permitted the privilege of superseding the Constitution. Moreover, if even those who currently enjoy the privilege of religions personal laws wish to be governed by uniform criminal laws, there can be no justification for avoidance of a uniform civil code. To avoid this crucial issue any further is fraught with grave consequences for the country's polity and the very notion of secular democracy.

The issue of a uniform civil code is understandably debatable and controversial, but also unavoidable. Article 14 of the constitution requires the government to implement a uniform civil code, although this was enshrined not as a Fundamental Right, but a Directive Principle of State Policy, and therefore not justiciable in courts of law. Successive governments, which have been prodded by the courts of the country to implement a Uniform Civil Code, have chosen to evade the issue, the foremost reason being keeping a captive vote bank firmly within their grasp. Jawaharlal Nehru's refusal to even touch the question of reform among other communities while pushing the Hindu Code Bill makes it very difficult to deny this charge.

It needs no reiteration that laws have to be equal for all citizens, irrespective of religion, caste or gender. This is particularly so far a country that also calls itself democratic and a secular democracy on top of it. In other words, the need for a uniform civil code flows from the very concept of secularism, which mandates the complete separation of religion and state. The argument that such a rigid divorce of faith and state is a Western idea and construct does not hold any merit here. Even if one were to argue in favour of an Indian variant of 'secularism', i.e., equal respect for all faiths, the present Indian Constitution's permitting personal religious laws to prevail for the Muslim community in the matter of marriage and divorce is an unambiguous violation of the stated Constitutional right of equality as laid down in Articles 14 and 15.

* * *

12. INDO-PAK CLASHES ARE CIVIL, NOT INTERNATIONAL WARS

A number of Indians have written articles celebrating the country's joint victory with Bangladesh in 1971. I have no quarrel in principle with commemorating any triumph including one on the cricket or hockey field. Although a victory over Pakistan is an intra-sub-continental affair and therefore, rather like a para-civil war and not an international triumph. We have not enjoyed such an achievement since Chandragupta Maurya defeated Seleucus the appointee of Alexander (the great) over Bactria in the 317 BC.

That is a quibble contrasted with the blunder of helping to separate the eastern wing of Pakistan from the rest of the country. International *real politik* would have suggested that the eastern wing with a majority of the country's population was a mill-stone round Pakistan's neck. First and foremost, the population of the eastern wing was greater than that of the western. Secondly, the Bengalis appeared prouder of their language than their religion whether Islam or Hinduism. In fact, Bengal was a reluctant applicant to Pakistan. Fazlur Rahman and Sir Abdul Rahim were negotiating with Sarat Bose to keep the province united to be a third separate dominion over and above Hindustan and Pakistan. Jinnah was encouraging them because a Muslim majority dominion would mostly side with Pakistan, especially with a Muslim premier forever. The Communist Party was also backing this third opinion.

What East Bengal—now Bangladesh—meant to Qaid-e-Azam Jinnah is reflected in the fact that he had never visited it before March 1948. When he did visit, he addressed the Dhaka University only to tell its students that Urdu would be the sole national language of Pakistan, angering his audience. Jinnah arrived in Dhaka on March 19th, 1948. On March 21st, he warned a large crowd at the Dhaka Race Course, against what he called the forces of subversive conspiracy bent on destroying Pakistan's unity. Feeble protests were heard from the crowd. Far louder voices of protest were to be heard only days later. The Qaid had through his Dhaka speech set East Bengal on a course that was to lead, over the next 24 years, to the break-up of Pakistan and the rise of East Bengal as the independent republic of Bangladesh.

Moreover, Ayesha Jalal, the Cambridge scholar who has authored a volume entitled *The Sole Spokesman*, called the East Pakistan a rural slum, meaning worthless except for growing rice, which the locals ate up, and raw jute with no mills which could weave them until later. And of course, in the Sylhet district there were some tea plantations. But it must be said that the jute and tea earned some hard currency foreign exchange, more than what the western wing earned in 1947/48. Nevertheless the tall, fair west Pakistanis looked down upon the easterners as dark, short and inferior. The least one did was to look upon the New Medina *walas* (Aligarh University students) where the sub-continental 'brotherhood of Islam' were to gather. In that potential fortress of Islam, could one momin look at another momin of the east with such contempt? Yet he did until he was rid of the dark, short brother/sister in 1971, in his heart of hearts good riddance.

West Pakistanis were smug besides being contemptuous. One example was the Field Marshal Ayub, at the peak of his power, amalgamated all of west Pakistan into one province with Khan Saheb, the brother of Frontier Gandhi, as the chief minister. He called it the province west Pakistan. Instead, he should have sub-divided east Pakistan into say four provinces. So that the eastern wing would have united to vote for Awami League in 1971 and won all the seats except two and be in a position to vote out the whole of the western wing. The crisis had thus begun with Mujibur Rahman claiming to be prime minister-in-waiting. How can short, black people rule over the tall fair people? The western wing considered this an abdominal thought and therefore sent Lt. General Tika Khan to devastate the Bengalis.

In the late 1990s and the regime of Begum Khaleda Rahman, Bangladesh awarded India with six chopped heads of it Border Security Forces on bamboos like shikared animals across the border. Indians were so dreaded that they took the beheaded heads of their soldiers with equanimity! There have been highs in Indo-Bangladesh relations in the years of Bangabandhu and these six heads on bamboos were the low. When Moraji Desai came to power in 1977, he said that we had one Pakistan but Indira Gandhi has given us two.

Our relation with Dhaka appears to be warm cordial since Prime Minister Modi came to power but recently Bangladesh rewarded India by desecrating 92 temples in their country and killing a few local Hindus. It is possible that the mischief was resorted to by one or more terrorist groups and had nothing to do with the majority party called Awami League. Nevertheless, the rioting proved, once again, that Bangladesh can prove to be, from time to time, a haven and a launch pad of terrorism. What did India gain by freeing Bangladesh from the yoke of Islamabad? If not infiltrators, terrorists?

* * *

13. ADVOCATE JINNAH, DOUBTFUL CLIENTS AND AN INDIFFERENT COURT

Mohammad Ali Jinnah, the Qaid-e-Azam of Pakistan, was in his career an advocate par excellence. Jinnah, in fact, was commanding the highest fees in all of the British Empire. And his advocacy touched the zenith in the one cause he so passionately and resolutely pursued—carving a separate state of Pakistan for India's Muslims.

Not everyone shared this passion. The Muslim majority provinces in India's northwest were not gripped by anxiety, as the community was already in a majority in those provinces, governed by Muslim premiers. It was in the provinces of India where Muslims were in a minority that they were anxious. How were they to cope with a dominant Hindu majority and acquiesce to being ruled by them? These provinces, unlike those in the northwestern part, were in the hinterland of India and could not be part of any separate state. The British had wanted a single country—federal or confederal—with a single army for the protection of their empire.

Centered at Aligarh, UP's Muslims were all for Pakistan as their New Medina. The Caliphate, the centre of Sunni Islam, ended in 1924 when Ataturk Kemal Pasha had abolished it and exiled the last Caliph. The Ottoman Empire was defeated and dissolved in WWI and along with it ended the rule of its sultan. UP's Muslims intensely campaigned for the 1945-46 elections, on the issue of a separate Muslim state, although UP could not join the northwest where Punjab and the North West Frontier Province (now called Khyber-Pakhtoonkhwa) are located.

The Khojas, Memons and Bohras of Bombay were supporters of Pakistan. They had their reasons for doing so. In an undivided India, they would have to compete with the Hindu business community. In a likely Pakistan, their only competition would be the agrarian community of Punjab. They were ready to finance the Muslim League's campaign, although were themselves not numerous enough to create a separate country.

Bengal had the maximum number of people but the province wanted its own separate *Sonar Bangla.* Fazlur Rahman, Sarat Bose and others negotiated for a third dominion, distinct from India and Pakistan. Assam had only one district of Sylhet. Punjab had been content for decades with the Unionist Party led by the family of the Hayat Khans. It had a Muslim majority and its own premier, with a coalition of Hindu and Sikh landlords along with Muslim zamindars. Moreover, the market of the whole of India was available for its produce.

Sindh had a Muslim majority, of farmers and peasants. The Hindu minority there comprised of businessmen, intellectuals and administrators, led by G.M. Syed, who later led the Jio Sindh secessionist movement. Jinnah wanted the province to be left alone for the time being lest it took a contrarian stand. The North West Frontier Province had a Congress minority regime of Khan sahib, the younger brother of Khan Abdul Ghaffar Khan, popularly known as the Frontier Gandhi. Balochistan, thinly populated, was a separate country and not a part of British India; it was the princely state of Kalat, with an embassy at Karachi until 1948, when its Bugti prince asked Jawaharlal Nehru to merge the state with India.

This was the baggage Jinnah the advocate had to deal with. Where was the question of any leadership? He had not travelled beyond Calcutta. His first (and only) visit to the birthplace of the Muslim League, namely Dacca was in March 1948. He had never been to Assam. He was not sufficiently familiar with Punjab or the NWFP. He had visited Quetta in Balochistan only for a holiday.

The Qaid-e-Azam was essentially an urbanite. His brother Ahmed, a close friend of my grandfather, told the latter during an afternoon chat in 1946 that they were not really Muslim. They couldn't perform the *namaz* nor had any Muslim attire like the *sherwani*. They ate and drank as they desired. They were actually Parsi in their lifestyle. Ahmed had married a Swiss lady while his elder brother had married Ruttie, the daughter of one of his close friends, a Parsi magnate. Jinnah developed a weakness to the pork sandwiches Ruttie made with excellence. Both brothers enjoyed their whisky. Addressing a rally in Jalandhar in 1946, he even smoked a cigar when his audience dispersed for a while for their afternoon *namaz*. None minded this indiscretion, as they were convinced that he was the messiah would deliver them their desired new Medina.

Where is there any quality of a genuine leader in all this? In fact, after the parting of ways with the Congress and Gandhi at the party's Calcutta plenum in 1928, Jinnah settled in London to pursue his legal career, buying himself a bungalow in Hampstead to live the English life he loved. He stayed in England till 1935 the Muslim League persuaded him to return to India to become its life president.

Jinnah's 1940 speech explaining the rationale for Partition also speaks of his resolve of finding a place in the hall of history, which was to be his fee for his successful advocacy of Pakistan. However, this was a fee the subcontinent's Muslims were to pay. This fee was for gathering support for Pakistan, putting it together, and obtaining it from Britain.

* * *

14. SALMAN KHURSHID AND HIS EQUIVOCALISM

Salman Khurshid's pedigree comes through in the book titled *Sunrise over Ayodhya*, only if one chooses to completely ignore his comparison of the Rashtriya Swayamsewak Sangh (RSS) with the Islamic State of Iraq and Syria or what is better known as the ISIS, and the African jihadi outfit Boko Haram. Both the latter organizations make no bones about their aim of exterminating all non-Muslims in order to establish a worldwide Islamic Caliphate. While Hindutva will not be weakened by such comments, such provocation indeed does pose some danger to the Indian Muslim in the urban street and the remote village. One is of course welcome to hold a different view, but I have Muslim friends who are clear that they agree with me. Nevertheless, well-to-do, rich and well-connected individuals like Khurshid may feel safe, but the poor, who are much larger numbers, are not so resourceful or fortunate.

Then there are loudmouth speakers in Pakistan who don't bat an eyelid in conflating a win in a cricket match with a victory for Allah the Merciful and Islam the great religion. They did not stop here; they expressed the hope that their sentiments have a resonance across the border. By that, they meant that Indian Muslims would join the Pakistani celebration of Indian defeat—all this outpouring in the actual and virtual presence of millions of Hindus. Imagine what anger the Hindus might harbour towards their Muslim brethren, which may turn into fury one day. The victims would be those residing in the jhuggi-jhopadis and not those patronizing Il Pallazos and Mehr Manzils in the luxurious locales of say, Mumbai or Delhi. Have some consideration for the ordinary members of yours. Do not try to instigate them against the Hindus; it won't be in anyone's interest.

Similarly, what do some Indian Muslims, even ten well-off ones, gain by comparing Hindutva to the Boko Haram and ISIS? How many girls have the adherents of Hindutva abducted? How many people have they killed, as the ISIS has done and is still doing? I cannot see the remotest connection. The Oxford-educated Prime Minister Imran Khan not too long ago, blithely declared that Pakistan has treated its minorities ideally and India should therefore, learn from Islamabad. I had long ago aspired to study at that esteemed university. Maybe I too would have also imbibed such precious pearls of wisdom.

The dastardly jihadi terror attack on Mumbai—better known as 26/11—marks its 13th anniversary on this day. That is sure to remind Indian Muslims how their co-religionists can threat Indians. Did Imran Khan mean 26/11 when he said that India must learn from Pakistan how to treat its minorities? What else can it be? Or did he mean terror attacks which in the Hindu mind are associated with Pakistani inspiration? Many in the world believe that what Aligarh's students in 1946 hoped would become a New Medina, has developed into a new factory of terrorism. All this is building up a great deal of pressure on Indian Muslims. One of its concrete symptoms is the latest present that Salman Khurshid has given India, namely a book.

Let Pakistanis not forget Bangladesh is also their product. Had there been no Partition, there would have been no Bangladesh. How much blood Lt. General Tikka Khan made flow in the erstwhile East Pakistan, we in India need to know. A local journalist, writing in Bengali, had said that Tikka Khan and Lt. General Niazi spilled more Bengali blood than the

Ganga and Brahmaputra carry into the Bay of Bengal. This may have been forgotten over the last 50 years, but not temples, 92 of which have been demolished by terrorist miscreants in the towns of Bangladesh, and the blood of Hindu Bengalis have been made to flow into the streets. This is the manner in which Bangladesh has repaid the blood of Indian soldiers who laid down their lives on the fields of 'sonar' Bangla in 1971.

As a result of the verbal gyrations of people like Salman Khurshid and Imran Khan, Indian Muslims have been rendered into walnuts, stuck between the two blades of a nutcracker. When one arm remains static, the other comes down, trying to split open the edifice and spill innocent Indian blood. What do our helpless compatriots do? My appeal is for a breather, if not a long rest. Do not wait for Delhi's handle to off and reenact a 1971 in the west what it did in December of that year.

That apart, there is another very sinister angle to Salman Khurshid's diatribe against the RSS and Hindutva. He has been a minister, former diplomat and an important figure in Congress regimes. His statements have let his mask slip, revealing a double-faced person. While he is very eager to paint the RSS and Hindus in sordid colours, one cannot recall him uttering a word of condemnation of either the Boko Haram when it abducted and killed girls for the mere crime of becoming educated, or the ISIS for its spree of jihadi terror across the globe. Shorn of jargon, one is forced to conclude that the Oxford-educated Khurshid's utterances are nothing more than an attempt to 'normalize' and justify jihadi terrorism.

* * *

15. WHO REALLY IS MURDERING DEMOCRACY?

There were repeated mentions of the 'murder of democracy' on the opening day of Parliament. The cause was the suspension of twelve Rajya Sabha members by the vice-President of India presiding over the house. The behavior of some of the MP's was extraordinary to put it politely. In my year in the Rajya Sabha such a scheme was unthinkable; times obviously change. The repeal of the farm laws so soon after having been passed was, to my mind, was a new peak of democratic step in my view. There is a saying in Sanskrit to the effect *kshama virasya bhushanam* or forgiveness is the ornament is the valorous. A variation of this wisdom would be a gifted retreat behoves the generous king. A mere politician could have suspended the laws and gone on to separate the farmers from the middlemen who feel the threatened party from the former who in fact were permitted to do what they liked; sell their produce to anyone including overseas, including resort the middlemen in the event of an emergency. How this is a murder of democracy, I do not know.

If the Opposition has any doubt with the democratic nature of the repeal laws, let us glimpse at the track record of Prime Minister Modi. The abolition of the Planning Commission on the morrow of his coming to power in 2014 was the big beginning. It was the control of national wealth which could be distributed at the will of the central government.

Every statement came up with a plan and its budget. The chief minister came to annually call on the vice-chairman of the Commission with a bouquet of flowers. No one asked questions except as a formality if the Centre was happy with the particular state. The two VIPs had a photograph taken with grins on their two faces and the CM returned to his state.

The grant was money for jam. The responsibility for minority the implementation of the projects was that of state government. For example, one of the proposals of the state was to build a bridge for Rs. 800 crores and it was granted. The CM and his side-kicks would have the foundation stone laying photographed for record. After that whether the state built the bridge or not was to be seen by the state. No one at the Centre need to bother about the state. On the other hand, the state could year after year debit in its annual plan the depreciation of say Rs 80 crores or ten percent. In short, the Planning Commission amounted to a gifting body; what the state did with the gift was at its discretion as is a birthday present.

The Modi government replaced the Planning distribution as well as the state Sales Tax with the Goods and Services Tax which mode the state independent of reliance on the Centre to distribute its annual doles. Every state was on its own feet plus the Centre having no discretion. It is based on the merits of each state's economy, it production, it service and so on. The Centre cannot deny anything to an Opposition ruled state or give more to its favourite state. Is that not very democratic compared to the previous arrangement? This is related to the main finances of a state.

I am alleging that everyone was corrupt but the scope at the state level was considerable. Take a Planning grant from the Centre and do not spend it. Equally, the scope for favourite was also substantial. Once in power at the Centre, a party could make a state the way it chose. I do not know whether Planning had any connection with the economic progress or its lack. But one thing is certain that no planned economy has reached the First World.

Only a democrat can face the public as the Prime Minister does on his *Mann ki Baat* programme. Anyone can ask anything and embarrass the respondent. The Opposition can have the mischief played; the respondent has to have a clan record and no skeletons in his cupboard. No previous prime minister has experimented with such open, public programme. The public, on the other hand, feels that the country's top leader is accessible to them. He does not keep away from the common folk. This means that the PM is not their indirect representative but a direct one. This is how the Greek city democracy began and is the ultimate is freedom and people's rule. This is unusual for a leader who carries the highest security risk in the country and perhaps is the world. He mingles with people when he campaigns in the elections. He spares no punches.

Parliament is essential for being enabled to remain in the limelight. To interrupt its proceedings is to cut one of the main branches parliament members occupy. Rushing into the well, in that sense is suicidal for the Opposition. I realized that it is very necessary for the Opposition to protest as obviously as possible, but not to provoke its adjournment. The members can draw public attention by, for example, wearing black, whether masks, clothes or anything else. They can also sit in the aisles instead of their seats, and so on. But they should not lose floor time, which in today's time, is televised. Another gain is avoiding the impression that MPs collect their pay but avoid work.

* * *

16. WHAT IS FASCISM?

Speech with knowledge is sermon while without knowledge speech is a pulpit. Those is Indian politics frequently use the word fascism to abuse an Opposition party or its members without the slightest idea of what the word fascism means or signifies. To them it is an abusive alternative of despot.

Benito Mussolini, who initiated the fascist movement in March 1919 at Milan and founded the party called Partito Nazional Fascista in November 1921; it is farfetched to have been abusive. Or, does the very word "Fascist" connote political derogation. Perhaps it does to at least some members of the Indian intelligentsia. This is reason enough to recapitulate what was fascism really means.

The word "fascio" means a bundle or a bunch implying unity. The movement was in response to the corruption, unemployment and the virtual economic collapse in Italy after World War I. The socio-economic conditions appeared to be ripe for a communist revolution and fascism was a nationalist answer to preempt such a take-over. Marxism was looked upon as depicting "class conflict". Capitalism still carried the stigma of "class exploitation" and was therefore a non-starter as a popular programme. To be effective the answer had to be something that would prove attractive to the peasants, to the workers as well as to their unions and generally acceptable to all classes of people. This was discovered in "class collaboration" as represented by fascism.

Prof Alfredo Rocco, the Minister of Justice in the Mussolini cabinet, set forth the gist of this new ideology in the course of a speech at Perugia in 1925. According to him, the society does not exist for the individual, but the individual for the society. Economic progress is a social interest and all classes of people should collaborate to maximize production. The interests of the employers and the employed are identical. To ensure that this is practiced, there must be a system of state discipline over class conflicts. Strikes and lockouts were alike illegal and punishable by heavy fines and other punishments.

Wherever possible, the employers and workers in each industry, trade or profession were organized together in syndical associations. Where it was not possible to form such syndicates, the unions and the employers' associations remained but cooperated to form guilds to coordinate and ensure cordiality. If collective bargaining could not end satisfactorily, the disputes were referred to law courts assisted by professional experts. This is how class collaboration was conceptualized by the Fascist Party.

In practice, the economy was toned up by rearmament and expenditure on public works. Soldiers were recruited in large numbers and so were workers in factories to produce arms. This would bring profits to the bourgeoisie who could then pay the proletariat well. Urban prosperity would increase demand for agricultural produce. What was left of the under-employed youth was absorbed by the armed forces. The promise to the whole nation were frequent attempts at foreign conquests which would bring booty.

Another example of the practice of fascism or class collaboration, albeit on a much more limited scale, was in Spain under Gen. Franco. Neither the Italian nor the Spanish experience is widely known in any great detail especially in

India. What however, the members of the intelligentsia are familiar with are the exploits of Adolf Hitler and his Nazi Party whose full name was National Socialist German Workingmen's Party. It was founded by Adolf Hitler and his six comrades in Munich in 1920. The economic deprivation in Germany was much greater than witnessed in Italy, mainly due to reparation payments under the Treaty of Versailles 1919 after World War I. The country paid an exorbitant price for its defeat in World War I. The runaway inflation as well as the world depression ignited by the crash in share prices on the Wall Street in New York in 1929 made matters worse for Germany. It was widely believed that the charismatic quality of Hitler and his programme of class collaboration more or less on the lines of Mussolini's Italian ideology, although on a far grander scale, saved the country from utter collapse and a communist takeover in the 1930s.

Unlike the Italian and Spanish examples, the Nazi Party proposed to exclude Jews from German life. They alleged that the Jewish leadership had betrayed the state during World War I and were to a large extent responsible for the dire German defeat. In their bid to exterminate the Jews, not only from Germany but also from the rest of Europe, the Nazis were estimated to have killed six million Jews by 1945. While Gen. Franco confined himself to Spain, Benito Mussolini did attempt foreign conquests of Albania and Ethiopia but his plans were nowhere as grandiose as Adolf Hitler's. Which is why he is so well-known not only in India but all over the world. Japan was another country, although a monarchy, also practiced class collaboration especially in the 1930s and 1940s.

So much for fascism and its smaller as well as grander (Spanish, and German) variations. But what is its ugly connection with politics in India? India is not Europe nor do we have class stratifications although communist trade unions did try to introduce them. The nineteen-nineties are not the thirties. Socialism is on its deathbed, and there is no fear of a communist take-over.

* * *

17. WORSHIP OF WOMEN

An Arabic proverb says, "Trust neither a king, nor a horse nor a woman". Another one questions "What has a woman to do with the council of a nation?" A third one says, "Obedience to a woman will have to be repented of" (*Dictionary of Islam* by Thomas Patrick Hughes; Rupa & Co, 1999). Prophet Mohammad improved upon such sentiments. Nevertheless, it is not easy to erase what has been part of a culture for long. As a result, even today, in any matter, if a man happens to be a witness, two women will be required to counter him, according to the Sharia. Which means a woman is half a person compared to a man. But in our subcontinent, we have worshipped *devis*—Durga, Lakshmi and Saraswati and many others. As far as I know, the pantheon of no other religion practiced today worships any goddess.

A possible explanation is that Hinduism has intuitively followed nature's trail of man and woman being indispensable for the perpetuation of the species. Hinduism is not the gift of any prophet, unlike most other faiths. Mostly, religions were founded by men who assigned a subordinate role to the woman.

Intriguingly, foreign faiths that came to India too have been influenced by the peculiarity of Hinduism. Devas and Devis both have to be worshipped, not just the male deities or messiahs. It is possible that other faiths have been deeply influenced or affected by the converts who came into their fold. This possibly explains why Bangladesh has had two women prime ministers, Sheikh Hasina Wajed and Begum Khaleda

Zia. Pakistan, with comparatively more imported blood, has had only one lady prime minister, Benazir Bhutto. The cultures of both countries allowed their womenfolk to reach the portals of politics, but not into the gates that may lead them to godliness. We can only hope that the era may not be far when this too will come about. A clergyman, I am friendly with, told me that this is very unlikely as it would threaten our god-given faith.

Upon arguing further, the clergyman was rather obstinate on the issue of women. My contention was that shutting out women means excluding half the population from participating in civilization's progress. If the wheel of progress is to move on as well as accelerate, such exclusion would mean the loss of half one's people. Having done so, one cannot complain that one's community is poor and backward. Prof. Timur Koran of the Duke University, USA, has dwelt at length on the backwardness of most of West Asia. What embarrasses me is that the community whose princes ruled large tracts of India should now claim to be poor and backward. Some speakers even compare the condition of their community with that of the Dalits!

Uncannily, the USA, the world's great democracy, has yet to elect a woman president. Only recently has a lady become the Vice-President of America after 240 years of the country's flourishing. This evokes the question as to whether female backwardness is an Abrahamic flaw, and not merely an Islamic fault? The prejudice against women however clashes with the current march of time. Women have progressed in many a field except perhaps in the realm of power. This is not to suggest that the current Hindu ethos merits unqualified applause. It too needs to lockstep with times and enable its womenfolk to attain and avail of a wider scope, without resorting to the escapism of reservations. Such marking out of seats has been an Indian obsession, which has not really taken anyone forward.

What is perhaps necessary is to create special opportunities for women to get better educated. Education, rather than reservation, may well be the key for women's emancipation and genuine progress, as compared to mere tokenism. Especially so, if an individual girl is encouraged in accordance with her aptitude. This lever of learning has not been consciously attempted even for the Dalits.

It is no mere cliché to state that empathy for, and acceptance of, women as equals in the endeavour of life brings about greater harmony in societies and nations. Setting aside the religious aspect briefly, we cannot overlook the fact that societies and cultures that have traditionally relegated womenfolk to a subordinate positions have also been less tolerant of ways of life that differ from their own. Historically, this has engendered societal tension, conflict and warfare, which humankind is still forced to endure and come to terms with. It is not a coincidence that the most debilitating projects of expansionism, wars and civilizational upheavals emanating from them have come from the western side of the world.

On the other hand, only genuine empowerment of womenfolk can achieve not only societal balance but also a civilizational ethos based upon empathy, which are natural feminine attributes. Nobel Laureate Amartya Sen's contention that education and health are the best guarantors of economic development is particularly relevant when it comes to the application of these two very crucial indices for women. It would be no exaggeration to state that it is here that the better half of humanity must be really worshipped, for the sake of not only democracy and progress, but for a secure future of human society itself.

* * *

18. PERSONA AND PARTIES MATTER, NOT ALLIANCES

Neither the National Democratic Alliance (NDA) nor the United Progressive Alliance (UPA) can keep any political party together. One of the reasons Atal Bihari Vajpayee lost the 2004 general elections was the projection of more of the NDA and less of his own party the BJP. The party cadres, who have been trained all their working lives that their mission is the attainment of Hindu rashtra, were not impressed. The party's name itself had undergone a change thrice; from the Bharatiya Jana Sangh to the Janata Party and then finally its current avatar the Bharatiya Janata Party (BJP).

So long as Hindu rashtra remains the mission, the cadre and worker know what to do. When they were made to listen to the symphony of the NDA, or "India Shining" and "Feel Good", confusion set in, taking Vajpayee to his political oblivion. His ego took refuge in the supposed cause of riots having taken place in one of the country's states. In actual fact, Vajpayee's successors rode to power twice in subsequent years. In the hour of the 2004 electoral defeat, it was rumoured that the symphony of the NDA had been orchestrated by Vajpayee and his minions; more so the latter, in order to distance themselves from the RSS and move towards becoming a centrist party. The Sangh for its part, had serious reservations about the proclivities of this group.

What was true of the NDA is also true of the UPA, albeit in a different way. In Indian politics, the name of the central party, which we may refer to as the mother party, enjoys brand equity of a high degree. If a central party has to enter into political alliances, every alliance partner reduces the goodwill and does not add to the mother party's prospects, or even image. The combination of two or more political parties conveys the impression the main party is weak and is therefore seeking the help of smaller constituents, some of whom are wont to do the disappearing trick the moment they smell an opportunity to further their own political interests. In the event of such circumstances, the cadres would be satisfied with even a subtle change of leadership. As my grandmother used to say, a daughter is as good as a son.

The loyal echelons of the mother party appear to be unaware of the enormity of the brand equity bequeathed to their party. There can arise situations in the life of a political party, causing much despondency, but there never need be undue defeatism. Downs are often followed by ups, and back again. One has to remember that the ruling party of today had managed to obtain only two seats in the 1984 Lok Sabha elections. Earlier, in 1977, the Congress had failed to win a single seat from Amritsar to Calcutta, in the elections that were held after the Emergency.

Politics is not a game of intelligence, but one of popularity. Rajiv Gandhi knew little important beyond gadgets and computers. Indira Gandhi had a political gut and the sense to seek expert advice. She saw no reason to strain her own mind. Her father Jawaharlal Nehru, on the morrow of Independence told General Lockhart, the interim commander-in-chief of Indian army, to make preparations to disband the Indian army; India's credo was peace and police was sufficient to take care of the safety of its people, he said.

Moreover, it should be realized that ideologies help to hold parties together, but do not necessarily attract the voters. The reason is that the country is large and diverse in so many ways that ideologies and manifestos are seldom read and therefore, have little effect. People vote for or against a personality, whom it is easier to identify with.

The Congress in its heyday certainly reflected this truth and even today, despite having its lost its primacy in the country's politics and become a pale shadow of its former self, operates on this principle. The Nehru-Gandhi dynasty is the be-all and end-all of its politics. There is absolutely no scope for any outsider to become the leader of the Congress. Many, from the days of Jawaharlal, Indira, Rajiv and the Italian-born Sonia have tried to, only to splinter from the mother party and fade out before too long. Some splinters have ended up as regional parties, but these two have survived only around one leader and his family, or a particular caste, whatever high-sounding ideological labels they might sport.

The BJP thankfully has eschewed the trap of dynastic feudalism, but nonetheless remains the mother party because of its basis in nationalism rooted in the country's civilizational ethos. Its brand equity flows from its parent organization the Rashtriya Swayamsewak Sangh (RSS). The core of the BJP's brand equity, as that of its parent, is their unequivocal commitment to cultural nationalism. The party has waxed and waned in direct proportion to its adherence and willingness to act on this ideological commitment. There have been occasions when ambitious politicians have attempted to split from the mother party to try their own luck, only to disappear into nothingness. India's voters respond to personas, parties and a core ethos, not contrived alliances.

* * *

19. AMBEDKAR'S CONSTITUTION, AN ADAPTATION OF 1935 ACT

Dr. B. R. Ambedkar was first a Hindu leader and then a lawyer, constitutionalist and finally one who did not want to die as Hindu. What the 75 year history has done to him is to convert him into a Dalit great man. The depressed classes needed an icon and snapped up the ownership of Babasaheb. Jawaharlal Nehru needed someone who could draft the constitution quickly enough and, if possible, one who belonged to a lower caste to enable the Congress to claim affinity with the downtrodden of Hindu India.

The latter role Ambedkar performed with aplomb by getting hold of a copy of the Government of India Act, 1935 and chiseled it to make it look like a constitution. He was aware that Nehru would insist on minority pampering and such other frills and icings. Along with the minorities, the secular Hindus swear by the national document while, at the same time, amending it one and a half times a year. By now it has grown into a jumbo 400 article mammoth longer than any other constitution in the world.

What is not popularly known is that Babasaheb Ambedkar's finest hour was in 1941 when his '*Thoughts on Pakistan*' were published, within less than a year after Qaid-e-Azam Jinnah orated on the essentiality of Partition on 22, March 1940 which incidentally is a master piece on his logic of the 'two nation theory'. One may not agree with it but its eloquence cannot be denied.

There happened to be an institution in 1940 called the Independence Labour Party. This ILP resolved to study Jinnah's speech and prepare a rational reply to it. A seven person committee was formed with Babasaheb as its chairman. They brought some remarkable answers. They assessed that 90 percent of the Muslims held sentiments favouring Pakistan and therefore the issue cannot be swept under the carpet.

The five Muslim provinces (which wrongly included Assam) Jinnah demanded did not want a Central Government because in 1940 New Delhi's annual budget was about Rs. 120 crores. All the provinces' budgets totaled Rs. 74 crores. The Muslim League view was where was the need for the Central or the New Delhi budget. It served to only protect the land or provided law and order to the country. The League felt that the Muslims could adequately protect themselves on provincial budget account. There was no need for a Central Government which the Muslims saw as also a benefit of Partition. Why spend so much to buy peace; they asked? Merely in order to replace the British Central Government with an Indian duplicate? While the present is driven by emotions, when the tempers have cooled for different reasons in the future, the Hindus would wake up and, for financial reasons, want to forego the Central Government. So why not now was a Muslim argument?

The counter argument was that due to the theory of Martial Races, in the Punjabi Muslims, the Frontier Pathans etc. were disproportionately higher than men from the Hindu provinces who were fewer. The taxes however came disproportionately more from the Hindu provinces. Therefore, the Hindus would have spent more money and got less in protection. Remember the Islamic tradition was that a Muslim soldier could not fight a Muslim invader. The Khilafat Committee had supported the tradition and the League had endorsed it. This was discussed and decided when it was believed that, sooner or later, Afghanistan could invade the sub-continent. Babasaheb had analyzed this defence syndrome with the help of data left behind by the Simon Commission. There were some areas which sent hardly any soldiers and other regions that offered most of the men. Punjab was represented by 86,000 while the Central Provinces, more or less, today's Madhya Pradesh, only 100. Babasaheb went on to use what must sound, at the time, a devastating argument: Hindustan, once divided, would not have a natural frontier. It is therefore wise to have one's enemies without than within one's borders. How far-sighted was the great man and how involved he was with the safety of Hindustan. He was a greater Hindu than he was merely a Dalit.

Dr. Ambedkar advised the reader of his book to read it carefully and reflect upon it. 'Let him take to heart the warning which Carlyle gave to Englishmen of his generation: the Genius of England no longer soars through the storms, mewing her mighty youth, much like a greedy Ostrich intent on providence and a whole skin? 'Initially Hindus took it as a case of political measles to which a people in infancy suffer but before long the illness goes away? A few Hindus took it as a permanent frame of the Muslim mind and not merely a passing phase. Those who were casual and short-sighted merely said 'You don't have to cut your head to cure your headache?' 'You do not cut a baby into two because two women are engaged in a fight with both claiming to be the mother'. These were some of the warnings of the great man. One wishes that such minds were immortal.

* * *

20. ENGLISH LANGUAGE AND DRESS BECOMING WORLD STYLE

President Biden is not being Russo-savvy when he asks President Putin whether the latter has any intentions of conquering Ukraine. The latter has, with a straight face, denied that there are any plans of an invasion. But there is an attempt to incite pro-Russian elements inside Ukraine to aid and assist a Muscovite takeover of the former republic of the Soviet Union, Ukraine, which went out of the Union in 1991, more or less, with 14 other republics. That was when Mikhail Gorbachev was the Russian President. From the Czarist times to the year 1991, Ukraine was part of the Russian Empire and 1917 of the Soviet Union. After leaving the Union, the relations with Moscow were normal but the Kremlin had fears of Ukraine some days joining the European Union or perhaps even the NATO. The current tension between the two countries is the result of Kremlin's apprehensions.

To go deeper into national psychology beyond the international politics, Russians like to be European and would like to avoid being called Asian. The first big act in this direction was the decision of Czar Peter the Great to build a city which opens to Europe, which was St. Petersburg, later called Leningrad and now Petersburg. This was in the year 1703. This desire is one of the emotional reasons for keeping Ukraine under Russian tutelage. Similarly, Russia enjoyed the overlordship over Belorussia, Lithuania, Estonia, Latvia and Poland; the last three were too small and yet Moscow went out to capture them. But for the crises of 1991, they would have continued to be parts of the Soviet Union. The same sentiments did not exist for the six Asian republics, now also independent since 1991.

The second factor bugging Moscow is the apprehension that, at some stage, it could lose parts or all of Siberia, which is vast (13 million square km), rich in resources but with a sparse population. And of course, its climate is bitterly cold. In 1969, the Soviet Union was forced into a mini-war with China across the Ussuri River. Strange as it might seem, the Soviet Union was defeated and lost about a hundred islands situated on the rivers Ussuri, Amur and Argun. That mini-war was a historic message that China was a living threat to eastern Russia. Siberia has very few people whereas China across the Usuri River is a region with people and more people with not enough land area. On the other hand, China is entirely Asian and therefore without any European complex.

Uncannily, the Turks suffer from a similar Euro-complex. It remained suppressed while the Sultans ruled in Istanbul. Before these Muslim rulers arrived in 1473, a lot of Turkey was called the Byzantium. Without needing any obvious clarification, it was taken to be European and its capital was Constantinople, the city the Sultans renamed Istanbul. By the measures of cartography, only 3 percent of Turkish territory is in Europe today; the balance 97 percent is situated in Asia. Yet as Byzantium, no one asked the question whether it was in Europe or Asia. It was a continuation of Greece with the city of Troy popularized by the enigmatic Helen.

The desire to be European lived on. When after World War I, Mustafa Kamal Pasha, the famous Atatürk, took over as the ruler of Turkey, he expelled the Sultan and exiled him. He asked his people, both men and women, to wear European clothes and adopt as many Western ways as possible. Their future lay in Europe and he exhorted them to look West. In 1928, over only three months, he abolished the Arabian script of the Turkish language and replaced it with Roman alphabets. He had the Quran converted into these letters. These two measures have endured until now. Atatürk introduced an English model of democratic political system which under the current President is fumbling.

Nevertheless, even the President Erdoğan tried hard to enable his country to join the European Union. Incidentally, Turkey is a member of the North Atlantic Treaty Organization (NATO) since its inception after World War II. It was therefore a deep disappointment to be not admitted to the E.U. If its religion is the European objection to Turkey's entry, it unlikely that Turks would gain admission into the club of Europe. For reasons of history, especially its communist past, Russia remains outside of NATO as well as the E.U.

The Euro-complex extends far beyond Russia and Turkey. It is not only confined to the English language in order to communicate with the rest of the world, but extends much beyond. The Japanese have gone over to western dress, first men and then women. After the Mao Zedong passed away, the Chinese too have gone over to Western dress. In language, both the Japanese and the Chinese are completely have already or are adjusting to the European style. But it is undeniable that Western attire and the English language are the preferred options in most countries of the globe, notwithstanding the fact Europe and Britain are reported to be on decline in the civilizational context.

* * *

21. THE CHALLENGE OF MATHURA

It was at the Conoor Club years ago that I came across Salman Sait. In the course of the evening, speaking chaste Gujarati, he much appreciated the cuff-links I was wearing. My instinctive reaction was to take them off and hand them over to Sait with my best wishes. When he hesitated and declined to take them, I told him that I had merely worn the cuff links, while you had really appreciated them and therefore they rightfully belonged to you. He accepted them with a couple of tears in his eyes, saying how thankful he was.

To climb from the ridiculous to the sublime, while hiding in a pond after his rout in the Mahabharata war, Duryodhana offered Yudhishthira the empire of Hastinapura. The latter's reply was: Dear brother is it too late now?

Sentiments of a similar kind crossed my mind on the terrace of the *Sita ki Rasoi* at Ayodhya on December 6, 1992, where stood the Babri edifice when the karsewa was on in full swing. Poet Mohammad Iqbal decades earlier had called Rama "Imam-e-Hind". That alone should have been sufficient for his community to gift the edifice to the Hindus.

Today, my mind has flown to the year 1192 AD, when Prithviraja Chauhan lost his final battle to Mohammad Ghori? The latter, in the company of Qutbuddin Aibak, was passing through Ajmer, when they came across a triplex of temples. Ghori was taken up by the height and breadth of the complex and asked Aibak to have the triplex converted into a masjid soonest. On my way back, I would like to pray at this new masjid, he said. The obedient slave that he was of Ghori, Aibak got down to the job immediately and finished it in two-and-a half days. Since then, the converted masjid has been known as the "*Adhai din ka jhopda*". Conqueror Ghori was satisfied that he had humiliated Prithviraja adequately.

Since those barbaric times, we have passed more than a millennium. Only idiots remain stuck and do not change with the sands of times. When the distinguished historian Sir Arnold Toynbee visited India to deliver the Maulana Azad Memorial Lecture in 1961, he had some wisdom to share with his Indian audience.

Arnold Toynbee said: "In the course of the first occupation of Warsaw, the Russians had built an Eastern Cathedral in the city that had been the capital of the once independent Roman Catholic country Poland. The Russians had done this to give the Poles a continuous ocular demonstration that the Russians were now the masters. After the re-establishment of Poland's independence in 1918, the Poles pulled this cathedral down. I do not blame the Polish government for having pulled down the Russian church. The purpose for which the Russians had built it was political and positively offensive".

There are several points to be noted in what Sir Arnold stated. One, that Warsaw was the capital of Poland and a prestigious city. The Russians had converted a historic church to an Orthodox Christian place of worship. Three in all the Abrahamic faiths, a place of worship is merely a prayer hall and not a residence of God.

In reverse, the people of Ajmer could argue that they had not destroyed any masjid, nor was the triplex of temples situated in a prominent place in the city. Ajmer was also not the capital city of India. Incidentally, the Abrahamic faiths, Judaism, Christianity or Islam do not believe in idol worship. To that extent, the Polish people were justified. Several churches in England have been sold by the local parishes and rebuilt as Jain temples or secular institutions. I can immediately think of a church in Leicester.

The U.S.S.R. converted many churches and mosques into departmental stores or municipal offices. I have visited three of them during a visit to Moscow in 1973. No one objected and it happened as though in the course of business. For such a thing to happen to a Hindu temple is like crushing the heart of the devout.

Times have changed in several ways. Firstly, the '*Adhai din ka Jhopra*' was a temple that was desecrated on the morrow of a Hindu defeat. Two, the sense of magnanimity, which is the hallmark of true royal blood, was not a virtue of Mohammad Ghori. He was a lowly person who had been pardoned the previous year after his defeat at the Chauhan's hands, but showed no conscience in murdering Prithviraja. Three, this happened a millennium ago.

I appeal to my countrymen to be a little more magnanimous than Ghori, as well as be realistic about human values today. Islamic rule was formally over in 1858 when the Sepoy Mutiny was crushed by the British, whose own rule in turn, ended in 1947. In short, Abrahamic rule has long flown away from the banks of the Jamuna to beyond the Thames River. In any conflict within India which may take place, it would be for the Indians to settle. The Islamic flag which had flourished for centuries was transferred by Qaid-e-Azam Jinnah to the banks of the Indus. It therefore makes sense for the citizens to wash their past sins with the waters of magnanimity.

* * *

22. WHY A JOINT CHIEF OF DEFENCE?

Several months after the conclusion of the 1971 Bangladesh Liberation War, rumours had begun to fly that, due to its success, the army might take over power from the then Congress government. Prime Minister Indira Gandhi was anxious for her own reasons. That Inflation was increasing if not raging which she believed, was a frequent cause for loosing elections. She therefore, asked General Sam Manekshaw to meet her. While chatting, she happened to mention rumours of an army takeover, and asked the General if he had any such plans. Manekshaw, with his wry sense of humour, reacted by asking "So?"

This made Indira Gandhi nervous, but eventually she got an assurance that Manekshaw had no such plans. This episode put a lid on the concept of the integration of the three services of the armed forces under a single chief of staff. Divide and rule through bureaucrats remained the system, whose seed had been sown by Jawaharlal Nehru, who was doubly convinced that he was right when Ayub Khan seized power in Pakistan in 1958. Nehru had apprehensions since the morrow of independence. At that time, the British interim commander-in-chief of the Indian army General William Lockhart, asked Nehru as to the scale and style of the army he would like the C-in-C to plan for. To this, the Prime Minister's reply was that India was a peaceful country and therefore "had no need for an army". The police was sufficient to protect the country. The style and scale therefore, ought to be to whittle down the army.

V. K. Krishna Menon, India's then foreign minister, Nehru's friend and guru on foreign affairs and international relations also believed that the armed forces generally were a threat to the civilian government of a Third World Country. He also believed that no Communist country would even attack India, because it was looked upon as a "fraternal power". The Chinese Communist Party by then was winning that country's civil war and was expected to defeat the Nationalist Kuo Min Tang of Chiang Kai Shek, which it eventually did in October 1949.

As time went on, the Indian government's policy was to appoint gentle and obedient generals as commanders-in-chief, soon to be watered down to Chief of Staff. Only when there were strong candidates who could not be superseded were less gentle generals appointed to the top post. Generals Thimayya and Choudhary were examples.

This issue of a joint commander was not only swept under the carpet, but was dug deep into its grave. It was publicly raised for the first time when the BJP first came to power with Atal Bihari Vajpayee as Prime Minister. After that, the idea was tossed about with the respect a shuttlecock deserves. It was not until the present Prime Minister took over in 2014 that the idea of a Joint Chief of Defence staff starting jelling seriously in political circles.

The late General Bipin Rawat was first elevated to the position of Chief of Staff. It is only when he retired that the post of Chief of Defence Staff (CDS) was created and General Rawat was appointed to it. For example, he was perfectly professional appointment.

It is just possible that if the CDS had been in place in 1962, the Indian Air Force (IAF) might have been deployed in Ladakh, Arunachal Pradesh or both. As it happened, Prime Minister Nehru was flabbergasted so much as to weep on the radio with the words, "Assam is in danger". The then chief of army staff General Thapar had resigned, while General Brijmohan Kaul had no combat experience. In the meantime, the Indian soldiers, sent up at the last minute, had hardly any woolen clothes while trying to fight at up to 16,000 feet attitude. The Sino-Indian war of 1962 was possibly the most amateurishly fought by one side in the history of warfare, whereas the invading forces were well-trained and better equipped. Such a one-sided affair might have been avoided, had there been more experience of generalship with the help of a joint command of the three wings of the armed forces.

A great amount of water has flowed in the rivers of Ladakh. Warfare in the modern age is a multidimensional affair with an awesome variety of weaponry. It calls for a great deal of knowledge and experience, which a joint command would help to provide with generals, including naval and air sharing thoughts and inputs together. The air force in a war has today become indispensable. The navy has become a combination of war in the air as well as water. Even the army needs its own aircraft in today's theatres of war. The outcomes that flow from these permutations and combinations are truly mind-boggling.

Military commanders have to be thorough professionals in their domains and not the personal choices of the Prime Minister or political leadership. This is particularly important for our country because its culture has traditionally, been inspirational as distinct from empirical. From mathematics to medicine, ancient India's contribution has flowed through inspired rishis as opposed to research, experimentation and debate. For example, the great physician Charak revealed Ayurveda without seeing the inside of a human body. Therefore, we emphasize that our appointments should be strictly professional; neither personal nor inspirational.

* * *

23. SECULARISM

After Prime Minister Modi's epochal visit to his constituency Varanasi on Monday, December 13, noises have been raised in the media that the "spirit of secularism has been violated". Article 15 of India's Constitution insists on equality of all citizens regardless of gender, religion etc., permitting no discrimination; yet Articles 25 to 30 grant special privileges to the minorities. There is thus discrimination between the majority religion and the minority faiths. The Constitution itself allows violation of its Articles; it doesn't stop at permitting Muslims to practice their Sharia (personal law), but also prescribes what is allowed to Muslim men and Muslim women. The former can have, at a time four spouses but the latter are allowed only one husband. Why?

Think of the crores upon crores rupees spent on the erstwhile Hajj subsidy. Ironically, the Muslim leadership itself did not want it since its distribution was a powerful lever of influence. No one contested its abolition when it happened. The Quran does not encourage Hajj done with others' money, as it becomes no longer sacred.

Secularism is a European concept. Until the French Revolution in 1789, there were three houses of the French National Assembly; the Lords, the Commons and the Bishops and other clergy. The Roman Catholic Church had considerable influence on the running of the country. Plus, Christianity provided the monarch with the ideology of reigning until nationalism came to the fore. That is why liberals pressed and strove for separating the State from the Church.

In India, the Church did not influence the running of the State which in any case, was ruled by Britain's civil government until 1947. The Bible's Old Testament makes it clear that to God belongs what is His and to Caesar, i.e., the earthly ruler, what is rightly his. Secularism or the separation of Church from State therefore stands on a firm and ancient foundation of the Christian faith.

In India, there are several religions and each had its own prescription. Christianity never commanded a large enough constituency. Islam is a comprehensive prescription of how to live, including the nature of the State. Qaid-e-Azam Jinnah declared that Islam and Hinduism are so different that they cannot coexist in one country. They are two separate nations and have therefore to separate, or the country to be partitioned. That happened in 1947 without an exchange of population, which disappointed most members of the Muslim League. Pakistan was to be homeland of Muslims; the Aligarh elite even went to the extent of calling their new homeland the New Medina. After the abolishment of the Caliphate by Turkey's Mustafa Kemal Atatürk in 1924 and exiling the Caliph, Pakistan dreamt of producing a caliph. Muslims in India formed the Khilafat Committee to pressurize the British to reinstate the Caliph. Gandhi even became the President of this Committee although Jinnah shunned it.

Under the proposal of exchange of population most Muslims in India were to migrate to Pakistan, while non-Muslims were to migrate to India. Such an idea was implemented by the League of Nations, the predecessor of the United Nations. In 1923, Christians in Turkey were made to move to Greece while Muslims residing in Greece to cross into Turkey. The scheme was executed diligently and without bloodshed. Dr. Rajendra Prasad, India's first President, wrote India Divided, wherein he suggested that the Muslims who could not move could stay back in India as aliens with visas issued by the Indian government. Jinnah had readily endorsed this proposal, but strangely Gandhi propagated that Partition had been a 'territorial' division and not a religious one. He iterated this to Dr. Syama Prasad Mukherjee and Rajkumari Amrit Kaur on January 29th, 1948.

The point is that most Muslims had voted for the League in the 1945-46 elections. The party, led exclusively by Jinnah, had a single point manifesto—Pakistan. On 14th and 15th August, when Pakistan and Hindustan were separated, the sovereignty and the Islamic flag had moved to Karachi en route a future Islamabad. With regard to the rights of the other minorities like Christians, Parsis, Jews, India has no problems. Christian activities do occasionally cause tension on the issue of the conversion of poor Hindus to Christianity, but this is periodical. Buddhists and Sikhs have complaints on religious grounds.

Hinduism is a faith more than a religion. It expects the Hindu to adhere to karma with its reactions, equal and opposite. This core belief is as close as possible to Physics. Even God, wherever He is, does not interfere in deciding the bhagya or fate of any individual. Each individual's karma is believed to be determined on the scale of his expected dharma.

A priest has a duty different from a soldier, a cook from a washerman, a king from a subject and so on. Every other consideration is left to the discretion of the individual. In fact, there are Hindus who are agnostic and even atheistic. Karma is each according to an individual and Hindus mostly unite only under a calamitous provocation. Hindu faith has no real connection with running of the State: Hinduism is thus, toleration personified. A discussion on secularism should be peripheral and should mostly unnecessary in India after Partition.

* * *

24. BIDEN'S SUMMIT

It is safe to assume that U.S. President Joe Biden had in mind only electoral democracy when he invited many a head of government to his 9th December Summit for Democracy. Prime Minister Modi made an appropriate point tellingly when he said that the democratic spirit is integral to India's civilizational ethos. Centuries of colonial rule could not suppress the democratic sprit of the Indian people. He avoided extending the proposition to a faith in the phenomenon of karma which is nothing, if not democratic, on a metaphysical scale. All humans have a fair and equal opportunity to be automatically rewarded with or denied a *bhagya* or fate commensurate with his/her karma without a divine entity, say God, having an overriding say in the *bhagya*. The belief in the operation of karma is like the law of physics that every action there is an equal and opposite reaction. This is a faith being as near science as yet possible.

Another symptom of Indian democracy is its history down the ages. Anyone who arrived whether via the Hindu Kush or Arabian Sea as the early Jews, or other traders, the Parsees, British and many others were welcome, or at least allowed to stay and settle on the Indian soil. No one was expelled regardless of his being cruel or kind.

The idea behind the open welcome to one and all was that the world was one family, '*Vasudhaiva Kutumbakam*'. One advantage of this policy—call it Indic—or conduct was that the culture-cum-civilization became resilient and, regardless of its disinclination to fight, survived against any number and kind of invasions. Few cultures could withstand it and survive. It began with the advent of the Caliph and his successors, from Arabia, on to Egypt and the Mediterranean countries certainly up to Spain. On the eastern side were Iran, Central Asia, Afghanistan et al., but, strictly speaking, not India. If conversions of the indigenous on any scale took place, they were well after the Islamic conquest.

After the Sepoy Mutiny was over in 1858 A.D., contact with Britain was reasonably close and frequent. As a result, India youth, even women, learnt the British ways of education, culture as well as socio-politics by the early years of the twentieth century. When Independence came, Indian leaders were ready to adopt electoral democracy as the means to choose governments, at the Centre and the provinces. We also chose a parliamentary system and not the American presidential style one although it would have been, more suitable for India. Every adult was straightaway entitled to vote; those with more education, property or influence could exercise the advantage in their profession but not in an election. This insistence on equality is a hallmark of true electoral democracy. With the passage of every election, the Indian nation has learnt to participate better. There have so far been general elections at the Centre while the states have also been disciplined in holding their polls. The only significant interruption was the Emergency imposed by the Indira Gandhi regime in 1975; it lasted until early 1977. It was unpopular because it was declared only with the intent of saving Mrs. Gandhi's hold on power. Except for those 21 months or so, India's record of electoral democracy has been commendable.

Even when dealing with Mohammed Ali Jinnah and the Muslim League at Partition, India's behaviour was, if anything, over democratic. In anticipation of the separation, Qaid-e-Azam Jinnah and his colleagues were insistent that all

Muslims should be facilitated to migrate to the new Islamic country, their homeland. They were at times so vehement as to insist that all-Muslims should migrate to India. In his rabid enthusiasm, one the League bigwigs Sir Firoz Khan Noon thundered in February 1946 at Patna that if the Hindus in India came in the way of the transfer of Muslims to Pakistan, the League would re-enact the orgies of Chengez Khan and Hulagu Khan.

Indian leaders remained calm and implied that Muslims were also their brothers and they should be allowed to decide for themselves. An Exchange of Population plan was proposed and supported by Jinnah; whereby Muslims, preferably all of them, would migrate to Pakistan. And reciprocally, all non-Muslims would transfer to India. Dr. Rajendra Prasad, who subsequently became the President of independent India, wrote a book entitled *India Divided* wherein he suggested that those Muslims who not emigrate could stay in India as aliens with visas issued by the Government of India. The same could be done by Pakistan to the non-Muslims who remained behind in that country.

Jinnah promptly agreed with Dr. Prasad. Yet, the other Congress leaders kept quiet. In the end, Pakistan, with the help of violence, loot and killing chased out most Hindus whereas Muslims were allowed to stay back if they wished. Some went away from East Punjab (India), UP and Bihar but compared to Pakistan, India did practically little. This is true to this day, 75 years later.

This was the practice essence of the democracy. It is difficult to think of any other example of such devotion to freedom! India is indeed the land of freedom, and therefore democracy.

* * *

25. THE UMMAH AT A CROSSROADS

My sympathies go out to some of my Muslim friends who have been true *momins* and have lived through their religion, which is now approaching an era of flux. On the one hand, the Saudi Prince of Wales, Mohammad bin Salman, or MBS, as he is known by his acronym, has abolished Friday as a day of rest and prayer. The entire Abrahamic world has had a tradition of allotting one fixed day of the week as a day of Sabbath since the time of Prophet Abraham. The great man asked the Jews to rest and pray only on Saturdays, and not work. When Christianity appeared on the world stage, the apostles chose Sunday. The Muslim Caliphs were taken up with Friday and with afternoon prayers, accompanied by the *khutba,* which the imam delivers to communicate with the worshippers, standing on the steps called the *mimbar*. In the pre-technological era, this was about the only means of communication between the leaders and the followers.

With the advent of technology, the *khutba* is no longer indispensable. So presumably believes Prince Salman of Saudi Arabia. He has abolished Friday as the weekly holiday in his country. The *Jummah,* after which many a grand mosque has been named. Women are now free to drive cars in the kingdom; unmarried couples are free to occupy hotel rooms. The Sharia has been amended whereby minors will no longer be punished with death for any crimes. Flogging too, has been replaced with prison time, fines and community service.

Salman's Saudi Arabia is home to the Hejaz where Mecca and Medina are situated. One must remember that the king of

Saudi Arabia is the guardian of these two holy places. The lid on *taqlid* or orthodoxy, which was placed some thousand years ago is off. The era of reforms has begun to take off.

One leader who violated *taqlid* and subjected his country to drastic reforms was Mustafa Kemal Pasha, popularly known as Atatürk. He came to power in Turkey soon after World War I ended. He saw and said to his people that Turkey's future lay with Europe. He exhorted his country's menfolk to dress in lounge suits and womenfolk in skirts and blouses. He abolished the Arabic script for the Turkish language, all in a matter of three months. The Quran was re-written in the Roman script, just like the Turkish language. Kamal Pasha introduced Western-style democracy, replacing the Ottoman autocracy. Atatürk's vision has sadly, not been followed by the present ruler Erdoğan, consequently Turkey's dream of being admitted into the Europe Union and becoming a Western country have crashed.

In contrast to the tale of reform told above, our neighbours Pakistan and Bangladesh, especially the former have chosen orthodoxy, if not also obscurantism, as their pathway to destiny. Both call themselves Islamic republics and both desecrate, demolish temples as though they are diming with Emperor Aurangzeb. These two states came together, separated from India in 1947, to about turn to fall apart from each others in 1971. We still wonder what happened to the Two-Nation Theory—Hindus and Muslims – so eloquently advocated, first by Sir Sayyid Ahmad Khan, seconded by Poet Mohammad Iqbal and taken to its climax by Mohammed Ali Jinnah. That Muslims are one people was exploded by the Mukti Bahini of Bangladesh.

Abrahamism needs a CT scan to know why Judaism, membered by arguably the most brilliant in people the world, has shrunk so exponentially. Why has Christianity scattered into so many denominations as well as lost some of its followers very perceptibly in Europe? Why Islam antagonized so many countries in five of the six continents? Arguably the fourth sibling, Marxism, packed its bags so hastily. Life's but a walking a walking shadow, a poor player; that struts and frets his hour upon the stage, and then is heard no more. It is a tale told by an idiot, full of sound and fury, signifying nothing. Had William Shakespeare been commenting on the Abrahamic ideologies or outlooks, these famous lines of his would aptly describe them.

A British visitor once tried to explain to me that anything which is rigid is apt to crack and break, as communism did. Anything firm on the other hand, tends to scatter. Anything that does not change with the sands of time is apt to shrink. When frustrated with changelessness, some people cry out to quit their faith. Filmmaker Ali Akbar of Kerala is one such who has quit. As a good Indian, he could not bear the sight of people smiling at the recent helicopter crash over the Nilgiris. This phenomenon of smiling at such a national tragedy indicates that there are young men and women in India who feel happy when the country suffers a misfortune. They were possibly there in the days of Dr. Babasaheb Ambedkar, who incidentally, did not wish to die as a Hindu. He therefore, had to convert to another religion long before the day of his death. When he began thinking, he summarily put aside Christianity and Islam. Ambedkar said that since these faiths had been born outside Indi, they might have a denationalizing effect on his followers. His choice eventually fell on Buddhism. A person quitting his or her religion is a deserter who is called a *murtad* (apostate) who deserves the punishment of death.

* * *

26. INEQUALITY

The World Inequality Report 2022 has been published. French political economist Thomas Piketty and his team have reportedly brought forth a goldmine of data and what they claim several insights into this egregious problem. Christians are especially concerned with inequality and its corollary namely poverty. The deprivation of poverty is indeed one of worst curses on humanity, and perhaps also on animals, although a lot of it goes unnoticed. Or probably animals move away or migrate to greener, richer areas if they can. To move away is not always possible for humans who have to cross national boundaries.

Speaking as a believing Hindu, inequality is caused by the person's or people's karma, whether in this life or an earlier one. Foreigners, especially from the West, while visiting India are horrified by the sight of poor localities and the shanties therein. If one goes to speak to the poor people to ask them why they are so poor, the frequent reply is likely to be 'what to do Sir, (or Madam), my karams must have been bad. Now I cannot change them'. In Christiandom, the belief is that God created men equal but society has rendered them unequal. Bernard Shaw, the distinguished playwright called the poor casualties of civilization. He thus blamed society for the inequality, which in turn causes poverty.

Karl Marx was the product of his witnessing inequality resulting in acute poverty, which became more and more visible as industrialization advanced. Poverty was not so visible in the villages because it was scattered, although inequality was sharper in the rural areas. The difference between the lord and the serf in the standard of living was generally very acute. But ideologues like Marx had no facility to travel in the villages to study the economic life in the rural areas. Which partly explains why communism has not been considerate to poor peasants; its regimes dispossessed them and collectivized their minimal portions of land. The communist leaderships have been obsessed by the proletariat and Marx's Communist Manifesto called for the workers of the world to unite; there was no mention of the peasants in this all-important call.

In any case, communism killed itself rather than prosperity, poverty or inequality. One clear conclusion one can draw is that the ideology failed and its practioners met their demise primarily because the problem of inequality was insoluble. This is an indication that the theory of karma stands vindicated. Look at the large number of Christians, rather Jesuits, who have spent their lifetimes trying to teach in schools and cure the poor in hospitals but have not been able to crack the problem of poverty. Instead of curing inequality or poverty, they have succeeded only in converting millions of poor to the worship of Jesus Christ. They have not been able to solve any problem other than their utilization of economic activity to creating socio-political tensions.

If economic theory, political activity socio-religious service has failed to knock the bottom out of inequality, what can? There is a family of two brothers who inherited vast fortunes from their father. One brother has grown richer while the other is comprehensively bankrupt in a matter of a decade and a half. How does one explain such a phenomenon except with the help of karma? A learned Englishman has recently suggested democracy as a cure for inequality. As a last resort, he prescribed the removal of social barriers erected by caste, religion, ethnicity and gender, which should help to reduce inequality. Many a society in Europe had none of these barriers except gender, and yet the problem has persisted. A combination of democracy and socialism had been tried by Jawaharlal Nehru. It did not touch inequality; but it induced tax evasion and the illegal remittance of money out of the country to banks in countries that are tax havens.

The Scandinavian countries as well as Switzerland have got as near as abolishing poverty as presumably possible; but that is not equality. Those who wrote the Constitution of India did not come to grips with this subject. They wrote Liberty, Equality, and Fraternity at its beginning. The country was divided and re-divided but that has not brought about fraternity. There is tension, violence and killing in all three parts. There is about as much liberty that was separated in 1947, as anywhere in the world, although differences of opinions persist between the Opposition and the ruling party. India is a free country if a citizen is not a criminal, whether socially or as a result of his/her ideology. However, liberty does include the freedom to perform as much good karma as one can. There is no lid on karma as there was attempted on income in Nehru's India. If there cannot be a lid on karma, how can there be equality? Because not everyone can excel and be equal in the performance of good karma. If that be so, our last postulate, and that of our Constitution makers, collapses. No hope of equality! The reality of karma allows genuine liberty to the living being, but with attendant responsibility of the wisdom of choice. However, there is no scope for artificially enforced equality, whose outcomes have always been very debilitating.

* * *

27. WHY TOLLYWOOD LANGUISHES?

Mati-ul-Islam, a right-hand man of Sheikh Mujibur-Rahman and later finance Secretary of Bangladesh, first met Satyajit Ray in order to import some films for the benefit of Bangladeshis. The prices paid would astound listeners today. The maximum paid was *Apur Sansar*—the handsome price of Rs. 25,000/-. In all, he purchased twelve films. This incident apart, the Bengal film industry, popularly called Tollywood, has not marketed its products as profitable as it might have. Or conversely perhaps, it has produced what is intellectually attractive but commercially not much viable. Uncannily, Bengali men and women, in most segments of Bollywood have played a role as big as any other community, including setting up studios. Bombay Talkies was founded by Devika Rani and her husband. Her role cannot be underestimated when one realizes that Dilip Kumar aka Yusuf Khan was her exclusive find.

Bengalis sent nightingales, men and women of distinction to the song and music world of Bombay, most notably Hemant Kumar, Manna Dey and the inimitable Kishore Kumar, not to forget Geeta Roy (later Geeta Dutt) and the veteran Juthica Roy, who rendition of *Ghoonghat ke pat khol re tohe piyaa milenge* resonates even today. We cannot also forget that the immortal K.L. Saigal was a product of New Theatres, founded by B.N. Sircar. So were Saigal's renditions *Babul mora* and *Jab dil hi toot gaya,* which still ring in our ears. Incidentally, Saigal had been singing Rabindra *sangeet* in Kolkata. The golden voice of ghazals in the Bombay film world, Talat Mehmood too began his career in All India Radio, Calcutta under the pen name of Tapan Kumar.

One could conclude, and not without justification, that Tollywood has had talent but little success. The directors and filmmakers that come to mind are many, but let us mention the legendary Bimal Roy (who gave us *Do Bigha Zameen*, *Kabuliwala* and many other classics of Indian celluloid), Hrishikesh Mukherji, Basu Bhattacharya and Shakti Samanta among the prominent ones.

It is true that Tollywood has produced some Hindi and Urdu films such as *Devdas*, but the net cast by Bengali directors has been narrow and confined mainly to Bengali movies. By the same token, not many non-Bengalis got much space on the Tollywood screen. The reason is that unless one is a son of the soil, it is difficult to pick up spoken Bengali, which is first a melody and then a language. For example, one is pronounced 'Ayk' while twenty-one is 'ek'; 51 is 'ek anno' and 61 becomes 'ek sutti'. Not many who are not born in Bengal can cope with this variation of melody first and language later. Even those born on its soil are not conscious of this variation. As a result, once Bollywood got going, Tollywood could not compete. Also, Tollywood select subjects without any marketing strategy, and lacks a proper distribution network. The West Bengal government is silent about promoting good cinema while other state governments purse this seriously.

Another reason may be that Tollywood did not traverse from the zamindari psyche to that of businesspeople and eventually to the respectable middle class. The Bengali zamindar, once zamindari was over, continued to look down upon business as an OBC occupation; he descended straight into the middle class. The contempt for business persisted as before. Occupationally, the zamindar took refuge in either intellectualism or trade unionism.

When it came to films, Tollywood's scriptwriters and directors produced 'pure' and intellectual films, without any *masala* being allowed to touch the *kadhai,* a la Satyajit Ray, Ritwick Ghatak and Mrinal Sen. Anyone who could deal in *masala* stuff and wanted to make money had to take a train of the erstwhile Bengal Nagpur Railway (BNR) to Bombay.

It is not too late for Tollywood to catch up. For this, the Kolkata film world needs to think anew, devise new strategies and join the race. The normal or run-of-the-mill explanation of financial paucity would not come in the way. As the American businessmen say, "Money follows a bright new idea with the confidence to manage it. Ideas and management do not follow money". To take an example of a film that was a simple idea, which was followed by plenty of finance, it was *Gandhi* by Sir Richard Attenborough. From the most elderly and learned intellectuals to the youngest of school children, everyone could identity with the classic movie and enjoy it. Why did we have to wait for an English knight to produce a classic on an Indian giant?

Between the 19th and 20th centuries, India produced any number of giants. The saga of Netaji Subhash remains an epic, for instance. Gurudev Rabindranath Tagore was poetry and music personified, besides being India's first Nobel Laureate for Literature, for his *Gitanjali.* Bankim Chandra was an inspiration for heroes, for Tollywood or any other Wood to produce movies on. Ramakrishna Paramahansa and Vivekananda are spirituality epitomized.

Coming to themes, is there any shortage in West Bengal or any other part of India? Sadak Phu, the Sunderbans with its Royal Bengal tigers, the collieries and the tea gardens are landmarks of the state. *Kapurush* deals with tea gardens, but not with tea-growing; they use these gardens as a stage for a dubious romance.

* * *

28. EMPHASIS ON OFFENCE AND NEGLECT OF DEFENCE

It is a military axiom that an offensive military operation generally costs thrice the blood, money and resources that a defensive one does. Yet, conquerors—ambitious and impatient as they usually are—do not wait long enough for an adversary's provocation to attack. In the last century, Adolf Hitler was an outstanding example of not being patient enough to wait for the enemy to attack first. In the 19th century, Napoleon Bonaparte was a similar case. Napoleon and Hitler met with defeat; the latter also with death. In Hitler's case, a lady crystal-gazer predicted that he had to fulfil his military ambitions by 1943. Thereafter, her crystal showed a dark curtain. Hitler too had declared on Radio Berlin that he would rather fight in his forties than wait till his fifties.

Training and sustaining a soldier are expensive. Added to this expenditure is the humanitarian factor like the life of one's brethren who have volunteered to defend one's country. Incidents of our country's soldiers falling in action make most Indians grieve. Our latest experience has been the tragic death of Chief of Defence Staff General Bipin Rawat and twelve others in a helicopter crash in the Nilgiris; the nation was shaken. Emotion of this intensity might not be seen or felt if an air force plane crashes or a naval ship sinks; as did *INS Khukri* in the 1971 war.

Most countries term their functionaries in charge of the military forces as Ministers or Secretaries of Defence, although in a few nations they are known as Secretary of War; the United Kingdom in WWI, for instance. This might be because of the implicit embarrassment of a minister being proudly called a warmonger. Yet, right through known history, greater attention and expenditure have been devoted to killing enemy soldiers than to protecting one's own soldiers. The sword and the spear cost more than the shield. In the centuries gone by, there were no medics in the event of injuries to soldiers; nor was an ambulance available to salvage the wounded soldier. The *Stanford Encyclopedia* informs us that the system of organized medics began in the 19th century during the Napoleonic Wars. For the animals—mainly horses—in Europe and also elephants and camels in India, there was never any medical facility until their deployment in war died out.

The advent of gunpowder and later the innovation of the field gun, a revolutionary weapon again an offensive one, was more damaging to the enemy, but of no protective utility to one's own soldiers. The musket was actively used in Spain in the Battle of Parma in 1521, with its design undergoing improvement to transform into the modern rifle, in which the cartridge travels in a groove. This was developed in the 19th century based on the mechanics conceived of by English mathematician Benjamin Robins. It was entirely an offensive weapon. Helmets thereafter have become compulsory battle-gear for soldiers. The headgear is ancient but its consistent use began only towards the second half of World War I. The bulletproof jacket is not yet compulsory for all soldiers, although its use is now being increasingly mandated by Special Forces across the world.

The reason for such snail's pace progress in the evolution of defensive or protective equipment for soldiers must be sought in the mindset of aggrandizers and conquerors, who believed in and lived for conquests. Wars were the most potent means of attaining the political objectives of kingdoms, empires and later nations. Territorial conquests and continual expansions were the order of the age, for much of history. Soldiers were seen and treated as cogs in the wheel of a heartless machinery, or to put it crudely, cannon fodder. They came from the lowest rungs of the socioeconomic ladder and the incentive for the common folk to enlist and shed their lives—other than the undeniable attachment to one's land, religion and way of life—was also the promise of a share in the spoils of war. The last factor was particularly crucial for monarchs and adventurers wanting to line up multitudes of able-bodied men for conquests in faraway lands. Soldiers were meant to fight and die for their king, country or God; so was the thinking, which one finds prevailing till the 19th century.

Prince Klemens von Metternich, diplomat, statesman and Austria's foreign minister during the Napoleonic age, met Napoleon to try and persuade him to cease his quest for hegemony over Europe at the expense of human lives. Bonaparte's bland riposte was: "Aristocrats like you don't understand us soldiers born in the cantonment (Napoleon was born in one). They (soldiers) are meant to fight and die. I don't give a damn about them and neither do they". Things certainly have come a long way since those rather sordid days. The devastation of the two World Wars plus the possible horror of a nuclear holocaust, have certainly forced a sea change in the approach to conflict and warfare. While only the naïve would believe that war is a thing of the past, the technologies of the defence or war industry are undeniably reflective of increased concern for the safety of the fighting man and his individual and societal welfare.

* * *

29. ON CHINA

Since Deng Xiaoping's reforms, it was clear that the class profile of the Chinese society would change. A new bourgeoisie would emerge; petit bourgeoisie would enlarge itself with more money in its pockets. The proletariat would become prosperous. Perhaps the only class of people who could get left out of this economic revolution was the peasantry. When I asked my Marxist acquaintances to how the ruling party would remain communist and yet cope with the changing expectations of the people, their bland reply was that 'they will manage'. After all, many of the national assets are owned by the party; even the armed forces and the armaments are party-owned. So are the shares of the newly created corporations.

To someone like me who has grown up in India, it seemed a wonder as to how an ideologically dyed-in-the wool party can manage all classes of society. Evidently by force, was the answer I guessed. The communists reckoned there would be no problem since the Communist Party of China (CPC) practices politics which a typical Marxist does not recognize. A European professor had once explained to me the reason for this. The communist obsession is with the proletariat; the other classes matter little. The bourgeoisie and the landlords were marked out for extermination at the beginning of the revolution. The petit bourgeois should be watched and selectively also be exterminated. The farmers, other than the landlords, were the kulaks, peasants with limited land and have to be collectivized. The landless peasants willy nilly must join the communist movement. Inner-party democracy is all that is possible; this is at best collective leadership as distinct from the Führerprinzip practiced by the Nazis of Germany. At most, the entire communist party politburo might be consulted on policy.

Under democratic circumstances, a communist party cannot acquire or survive in power. Imagine Josef Stalin as a democrat. Or Mao Zedong surviving in a democracy following the famine of 1962, when 30 million poor Chinese starved to death. Or the Cultural Revolution when Mao stepped on and crushed thousands of toes? Leader versus leader is another level of struggle. Even Vladimir Lenin was shot at and wounded badly, evidently by a colleague or on his behalf. China was not free of such power play. The dozens of leaders and followers of Stalin exterminated through the 1920's and 1930's are legend. Leon Trotsky, Grigory Zinoviev and Lev Kamenev were only the top three. Stalin is reputed to have taken a toll of three million bureaucrats, army officers, farmers and members of the public. That was the way he lasted until 1953 when his more than 30 year innings ended naturally. Karl Marx appropriately chose the colour red for his cult!

Violence had to be adopted by the communists as a method of action. One reason was the lack of aversion to violence, the virtual opposite of Gandhism which was a mass movement comprising also of women, old people as well as children. The Marxist support base was a minority, namely the proletariat. Other classes of the people did not exactly adore the Marxists. A minority capturing and ruling over a large majority had necessarily to do so with an iron hand. Western Europe, especially Germany, Italy and Spain had to evolve a new ideology called Fascism to counter Communism. Originally, centered around class collaboration, fascism became a synonym for violent despotism. A red bullet had to be countered with at least a swastika and gun.

An autocracy, especially a dictatorship that traverses all aspects of life, has necessarily a short life. The Soviet Union lasted for 74 years. With its demise, it took along with it nearly all communist states, except North Korea and China. The CPC reacted with a novel experiment of continuing with the form but mostly abandoning its Marxist substance. If enterprises were promoted, their ownership was controlled with part ownership of the Party and not State. The armed forces are also owned by the Party. The leadership's insecurity has so far been assuaged by such ownership. True, the soldiers and sailors, as employees would fight for the Party and against its enemies. I wonder how well would they fight for the country against national enemies. Perhaps, the reason is that the nation has been looked upon as an adversary of the proletariat. Therefore, the Party General Secretary was more important in Soviet Russia than it prime minister. Josef Stalin remained the General Secretary of the CPSU (Party) till he died.

Chinese modernization after the death of Mao Zedong began with very limited capital. It insisted on the foreign entrepreneur investing everything, including his working capital overdraft bank facility. The local enterprise was financed by very cheap leased land and term loans to build the factory. When required, this money was printed by the State. If the loans were not returned on time, it was tolerated but the production had to be exported and earn up to 75 or 80 percent hard foreign currency. That explains China's large foreign exchange reserves abroad and banking crises at home. How to replace the printed money?

It would be interesting to see whether the yellow giant flourishes or falls in the coming years.

* * *

30. MARRIAGEABLE AGE OF WOMEN

An income-drawing girl began abolishing the need for her parents to pay a dowry, 50 years ago in West Bengal. This phenomenon must have spread to other areas too. Only a comparatively delayed marriage can enable a girl to get adequately educated to draw a lucrative income. That is where the introduction of 21 as the minimum age for marriage is an enabler. Although the current emphasis is on women, that an early marriage retards a man's studies is also a fact, perhaps more so because boys grow up somewhat later than girls.

The custom of marrying off girls young, in all probability, began with invasions from India's northwest, due to the rapacious lust of sex-starved invaders. Societal view was that an early marriage of girls would possibly distance her from the avaricious attentions of invaders. In Vedic times, for example, the custom was, at least for the upper classes, marrying off boys and girls at about the age of 25, because studies and learning for them were all-important.

Incidentally, the Islamic tradition was that a girl who crosses the stage of puberty is made her ready for matrimony. That is because of Prophet Mohammad's injunction published in the Mishkat-ul-Masbih: "Marry women who will be very prolific, for I wish you to be more numerous than any other people." Following this injunction may be appropriate for a community that does not encourage the employment of women. Such a practice excludes half the population from contributing to the national economy. There is another angle to this phenomenon, pointed out to me by one Anwar Ahmed, an artisan at Fatehpur Sikri; we were on our way to Agra. Ahmed's explanation for the educational backwardness of his community was that mothers in the community were comparatively lesser educated. He said an uneducated person couldn't know the value of education for her sons and daughters.

During my visit to Cairo in 1961, I came across a young lecturer at the Al-Azhar University. I happened to complement Europe's civilizational progress. To which his response was: "Wait and see; the next century will be an Islamic century. You will see signs of this in your own lifetime. Lesser educated women do not prevent men from studying and thinking."

Coming back to India, young marriages have caused more problems than solving any. The eras of invaders and conquerors are long over, but the adverse consequences they left behind remain unsolved. This is partly because India has been one of the few countries with mixed populations. The clergy, whether Deobandi or Barelvi, has been concerned that the youth of its community might be tempted to adopt secular ways and in the bargain, overlook the glory of Islam. Care should be taken to ensure that India does not fall into the trap of minority apprehensions retarding the progress of the entire nation.

Another advantage of a relatively late marriage of a girl would ensure better health for her; most likely because of her having fewer children. The step of fixing the minimum marriageable age at 21 would also affect the onward march of population amongst the minorities. If the clergy or the menfolk object, they should be shown the example of France. Until 1905, Paris allowed the country total freedom as far as one liked, worship the way one wanted and generally conduct oneself as one chose to. The country's National Assembly brought in a law in order to enforce secularism quite strictly. For example, no French citizen was thenceforth allowed to display any symbol of his/her religion outwardly, and certainly not while in public places, offices or institutions of education. A Christian could not wear a cross, nor a Jew wear a yarmulke, Muslims citizens of France could not wear a *burqa* in public; it was strictly banned in France during tenure of Nicholas Sarkozy.

Different segments responded to the message of the law in different ways. By now, the situation in France has gone to the extent that quite a number of mosques have had to be shut down by the authorities. Only a fortnight ago, a prominent mosque in Beauvais, just 100 km north of Paris was shut down by France's interior minister Gerald Darmanin. The imam of the mosque has been accused of propagating religious hatred against Christians, Jews and homosexuals through his sermons, called *khutba* in Arabic. Do we want such measures to be resorted to in India? If not, we must beware well in time.

We in India have witnessed innumerable communal riots, including what Dr. B.R. Ambedkar had described as a civil war, i.e., the clashes that took place between 1920 and 1940. Much worse was to happen thereafter in 1946-47 and in 1948 as well. Thereafter, we have seen four wars with Pakistan beginning in Kashmir in 1947. Today, India does not have a High Commissioner residing in Islamabad.

In 1971, the eastern wing of Pakistan seceded and became Bangladesh. This new country is more Bengali and less religious and follows the scriptures in a much lighter way. Bangladesh has controlled the excessive growth of its population, as well as perceptively improved its economy, to the extent that its currency the Taka is twice as valuable as the Pakistani rupee.

* * *

31. TAIWAN'S DEMOCRACY: THREAT TO CHINA'S DICTATORSHIP

Debates and discussions in Taiwan lately circle around the subject of democracy. The reason may well be the close proximity of this island nation to China, which claims the ownership of Taiwan. The intention might be to differentiate itself sharply from the communist dictatorship of the mainland; a subtle but obvious way of rejecting Beijing's claims.

China's apprehension would be that a successful democracy anywhere in its neighbourhood is a threat to its own system based on dictatorship; a growing bourgeoisie and an expanding petty bourgeoisie are themselves a lure for democracy.

In any case, in his heart of hearts, President Xi Jinping would know that his country had lost Taiwan a long time ago. Although the Chinese were aware of the existence of Taiwan and its native aboriginal population, Chinese settlement of the island did not begin until the 17th century. The Portuguese first visited the island in 1590, naming it Ilha Formosa (Beautiful Island), but were unprepared to settle there. By 1626, the Dutch and the Spanish had established fortified commercial settlements along the island's western coast. The Manchus began settling the island's eastern shores in 1796. In 1895, Taiwan was ceded to Japan following the Chinese-Japanese War.

Under the Japanese, Taiwan became a major supplier of rice and sugar to Japan. In the 1930s Japan's Taiwan policy turned to the development of industry based on cheap hydroelectric power. Following World War II Taiwan was ceded to China, then governed by the Nationalists (1945). Following the Communist victory on the mainland in 1949 the Nationalist government and its supporters, led by Gen. Chiang Kai-shek, fled to Taiwan. In 1945, the Nationalist government and the United States signed a mutual defense treaty. Taiwan has since then received military and economic support from the United States.

Taiwan has, even since the Communist takeover of China by Mao Zedong, been an eyesore for Beijing. This is understandable; Taiwan has not only become a highly developed economy with a sophisticated industrial and manufacturing base, particularly software and electronics, its close ties with the financial world of the West and the success of its democracy are a challenge to China's world view.

A democratic system is widely accepted as ideal; where it is not being practiced, it is because of obstructive vested interests, like those of potential autocracies or oligarchies. Or, the profile of the people is such that they are unable to organize a democratic system. The supreme demand of a democracy is the continual existence of at least a few leaders sacramentally wedded to rules that mandate that when one's time is up as President or Prime Minister, one gets up and leaves. Through modern history, the Anglo-Saxons are one people who have displayed this sacramental quality.

It began with King John of England, who signed the Magna Carta (the Great Charter) in the year 1215 at Runnymede (in Surrey). Since the sowing of this seed, democracy in the world has grown to become the rule of the people, by the people and for the people, as famously articulated by American President Abraham Lincoln (1860-65), one of the greatest democrats in the history of humankind.

This is not to say that other countries or societies do not have leaders who play by the rules. France and Germany are equally civilized but had allowed themselves to slip out of the lap of democracy. In an endeavour to push out the monarchical autocracy of Louis XVI that had lasted several years, France landed in the grip of Napoleon Bonaparte and his vaulting ambitions. It took a century and more for France to adopt a true and proper democratic constitution in 1905.

Germany adopted a democratic constitution in 1918, which fell apart with the advent of Adolf Hitler and his Nazi regime. Fortunately, two-thirds of the country returned to democracy soon after World War II, with Konrad Adenauer as its Chancellor. The other one-third had to endure a communist dictatorship under Herren Walter Ulbricht and Erich Honaker until communism and the Eastern Bloc fell in 1989.

Sweden is a constitutional monarchy, but only since 1921. Before that, it was like any other monarchy. About the only democracies in Asia are Japan and India. Otherwise, traditionally, democracy was an Anglo-Saxon monopoly.

Political parties that run a democratic system are broadly of two types. One type would be those with a virtually unchanging ideology, while the other type would have a view that encompasses the entire nation. The programmes or manifestos however, would alter with the wind. The latter type are the characteristics of Anglo-Saxon countries, with one exception. The British Labour Party remained fairly unchanged until Prime Minister Tony Blair innovated 'New Labour' in 1994, and ruled with it for the next ten years.

The non-ideological movements have the advantage of adjusting their manifestos every election, and therefore, do not get out of date. On the other hand, ideological organizations like the communist parties or the BJP can bend to the changing wind to some extent, but cannot violate their basic principles. When times change radically, they face the danger of expiring, as happened to the communist parties the world over. However, ideologies are excellent for binding parties and their members together.

* * *

32. CONSTITUTION NOT PANACEA; NEED REVIEW

Chile is rewriting its constitution, and the supposed reason behind such a drastic change is climate change and ecological crises. A climate and ecological emergency has been declared in this South American country; 155 representatives have been elected to write the new constitution. Chile wants to extract more of the soft shining metal called lithium, meant to be essential for making batteries for running vehicles without petroleum. This economic initiative will be part of the constitutional agenda. Chile has reserves of lithium more than all countries except Australia.

For decades, Chile has been somewhat of an outlier in South America, enjoying political stability and steady economic growth in a region that has been long mired in conflict and economic crises. But Chile's prosperity has been unequal, coming at a political cost, which is social inequality and friction. Proponents of the referendum envision a new charter that will enshrine more basic rights for all Chileans, especially free higher education and healthcare, as well as affordable housing and transportation, limit the role of the private sector, and expand public welfare to create a more equal society. They argue that while Chile's economy has been cruising for decades, growth has not trickled down to the majority of the people.

After decades as a regional model for political stability and economic growth, Chile finds it can no longer maintain both. Will the new constitution help the country's leaders find ways to maintain economic success while ensuring greater equity? Or, will this be a permanent tradeoff?

What is remarkable is that here is a country deciding to create a national document with a specific objective and not just a constitution. Most countries have produced their national documents without a specific agenda in answer to their nationally essential needs. When we look back 70 years and review what Indian leaders did in anticipation of January 26th 1950, we would get an example. They chose to carry on with more or less the system that the British rulers had used. That was introduced by the Government of India Act, 1935 to govern the brightest jewel in the British Crown more efficiently with greater powers devolving to Indians. At the time of its passing in 1935, the partition of the Indian empire was not envisaged.

How federal or unitary India's leaders would want their country to be, the British did not know. In 1946, a three-leader delegation called the Cabinet Mission proposed such a loose confederal map of India that the Centre would have only three subjects; namely, Foreign Affairs, Defence and Communications. The rest of the subjects would devolve to the provinces, as the states were called in those days. Their main endeavour was to keep the Muslim League happy without dividing the subcontinent.

When the leaders sat down to write the document, they had in mind the minorities, a federal façade but with a strong Centre to ensure the country did not break up. That explained the introduction of the Concurrent List of Articles, which dealt with those subjects in which both the Centre and the States had power. Law and Order is a State subject but the Central Reserve Police and the Assam Rifles established by the British respectively, were persisted with. And in due course, more paramilitary forces were added. Yet when inter-communal riots broke out, there were often demands for the military to be called out. In Gujarat, 2002, the demands were loud by the third day after the trouble began. The military did appear promptly; but then what was the Central Reserve Police for?

Just as Chile has an urgent need to extract more lithium from below the soil, our urgency in 1950 was to keep the country together in the face of its diversity, inter-lingual but more so inter-communal. In 1947, we allowed the partitioning of the country, losing some 35 percent of our territory. Within a few years, communal riots began. In Pakistan's western wing they continued until nearly all Hindus and Sikhs had taken refuge in India. From the eastern wing, there was a continual outflow because of bloodshed and abductions. Neither Partition nor the Constitution solved our central problem.

In 1781, the USA wrote a constitution which evidently answered the questions raised by its war of independence against the British Empire. There have been only 23 amendments over these 240 years. Our document has undergone well over a hundred amendments in the course of 72 years. On balance, the USA has flourished as a civilization; it is today the wealthiest nation and most of its citizens are prosperous. Certainly, its constitution cannot be faulted for any of its problems.

The Soviet Union wrote its constitution under the direction of Vladimir Lenin soon after the October Revolution of 1917. By 1991, the Soviet Union collapsed and scattered into 16 different countries. It was an ideological failure; Karl Marx overlooked human psychology that human beings must have incentive to work better. Equality might sound an attractive idea but people are not equal, and do not expect to be treated as such at work. Distribution of goods and services in a fair manner is important but their production is equally vital. The Soviets ignored this and perished.

* * *

33. CRICKET NEEDS MINDSET REVOLUTION

As I watched the second day of the second Test Match against South Africa, I found that the fast bowlers had not been able to take a wicket for quite a few hours. Yet none of them is able to try to bowl, for a change, with his left arm. Or try to bowl a leg cutter like Fazal Mahmood of Pakistan used to succeed in his day. Or even try a different type of slow delivery that Gary Sobers of the West Indies used to try when his opening spell was over. He was otherwise an opening paceman.

In the current competitive phase of cricket, why are there so few all-rounders? One of the few rays escaping through the clouds is of all-rounders, when there is sunshine of specialists. A right-hand batsman can be a left arm bowler. But he cannot bat with his left hand. Why cannot a left-arm bowler, slow, medium or fast, bowl with his right arm? The brain or the technology of bowling is one. The bowler is left-arm opener but he won't try his other arm when his left is failing to take a single wicket. The answer might be that he was not trained to bowl with both arms. True, but why cannot a young player of 22 make up by getting trained at this not old age? Is it his fear of diluting his expertise with his left arm? Or is it just plain mindset? Jaspreet Bumrah appears to have experimented with some batting lately. So probably has Mohammed Shami, although a little too late.

To say that India is a large country is an understatement and particularly so, when said in the context of cricket.

Australia, Sri Lanka and the West Indies are tiny by comparison. Yet each of them fields a Test team of eleven players; no more, no less. No nation fields, say, two or three teams. The same is the case with the 50 over one-dayer and the Twenty-20. In all, no country fields more than a total of 33 players on any one day. Sri Lanka with 25 million people and India with 1,400 million are weighed on the same scale. In the bargain, Indian cricketers are stifled with a miniscule scope for a career rise in recognized international cricket. One also knows that Indian players or their training academies do little to make youngsters more competitive.

For those young boys and girls who are ambidextrous, there are clearly five talents they could conceptually cultivate. This is batting and bowling with both hands and arms. Fielding is the fifth ability. Here too, why not learn to throw with both hands, which would make for a maximum of six faculties? If one goes by the example of Gary Sobers, there is the choice of fast bowling as well as slow-medium. This should be the simplest option.

This plea for all-rounders or versatile players is not merely for players and their training academies, but also for India. The boom in cricket began first with the introduction of 50-over one-dayers and a few decades thereafter, the advent of the Twenty-20 matches. Another great boost has been the innovation of the Indian Premier League (IPL) which has given a great deal of scope to young men all over India to obtain recognition and many of them to eventually reach the international arena. Without the IPL, a number of our cricketing flowers would not have been able to blossom so gloriously. The gardener who conceived of this League is by now unfortunately forgotten in some lesser known corner of the globe where he cannot be located and recognized! Indeed a great pity.

What we can apprehend is that in the absence of a continually expanding scope for players, they may at some future date consider emigrating to smaller countries. Suppose a small country like New Zealand runs short of talented cricketers, it might tempt a few Indian players to immigrate. I suppose there is nothing wrong with such a development. But I find it unwelcome if it is a result of our failure to foresee the future.

Something inexplicable needs to be mentioned here. And that is that certain tournaments attract crowds, while others just do not. Take the Ranji Trophy, named after the distinguished batsman Jam Ranjitsinhji, who innovated the behind the wicket stroke as a deliberate scoring attempt. Especially, the leg-cut, the sweep, etc., were not played until Ranji showed how, playing in England, mainly in the Country Cricket tournament. Even the off-side cuts were not very common; the frequent scoring style was in front of the wicket whether on the leg or the off side. Yet Ranji Trophy matches in India do not draw crowds. They never have, although playing for one's state should arouse enthusiasm.

In sharp contrast, the Pentangular and before it, the Quadrangular tournaments used to enjoy mass popularity. This was in the 1930s and 1940s. The latter comprised a Hindu, a Muslim, a Parsee and a European team. Thereafter, a Rest of India team was added to give Christians, Jews and others an opportunity. This popular tourney ended with rioting in many parts of the country followed by Partition. The 50-over one day internationals (ODIs) and Twenty-20s have revolutionized cricket in this context.

* * *

34. NATIONAL INTEGRITY COHESIVE PEOPLE

The anniversary of Capitol Insurrection—when an incumbent President Donald Trump gestured through an apparent revolt that he was not accepting the electoral verdict in favour of Democrat Joe Biden—is being discussed in the media today. Some writers seem to suggest that the Red states in the USA (Republican majority) could be prepared to separate from the Blue ones (Democratic majority). That might be a split between the Liberal and the Conservatives Americans, but is by no means wide enough to justify the breakup of the country. Lest one forgets, a bitter Civil War was fought for four years from 1861 to 1865 between the northern Yanks and the southern Confederates. Abraham Lincoln led the former with a missionary zeal, winning the war and preserving the Union, gaining recognition the greatest President of the USA.

It is however true, that being a creation of random immigration from the 15th century onwards, the USA does not have an integrated ethos. There are people of European, Japanese, Chinese, Korean, Indian, Hispanic, Arab and other Islamic origins. Most Indians do not raise their political heads. The others have a political muscle which they could use to further their cause. Indian-origin citizens, when they show up at cricket grounds in the UK, cheer the ethnic team, i.e., India, despite themselves holding British passports. Nevertheless, this is not a desirable symptom because it reflects that the nation does not have a single ethos and holds out a threat of a breakup which we are discussing.

But why go far? India has one single ethos plus several other political sentiments. Despite the partition of entirely religious lines in 1947, we are still religious factions whose ultimate loyalties are similar to those of Indians in the U.K. Unlike the USA and the UK, India has not undergone random immigrations. India's is a unique tale, which can be told by a historian who cannot justify its lack of an integrated ethos that can ensure national unity at all times and under all circumstances.

There are times when circumstances override national interests. In fact, until the end of the 18th and the beginning of the 19th century, there was little by way of a national awakening. If there was an ideology, it was either religion or language.

More than circumstances, the fault lay with the leadership at points of time of the countries concerned. Take France, for example. As a gesture of civilization, Paris declared its overseas empire to be metropolitan France. This made it easily possible for people from French colonies like Algeria, Morocco, etc., to emigrate to the cities and towns of France. Today, this European country has two huge segments of people, European and African. Being culturally and religiously very different, they find it difficult to coexist. Germany and Turkey were allies during the two World Wars. There were many Turks who did not have sufficient employment whereas Germany wanted cheaper labour. The former therefore arrived in droves to make Deutschland their home but Berlin insisted that they could settle only as guest workers, not as citizens. But what happens to children born to such guest workers? To add further to the population of Asians in the country, when refugees recently came rushing in from the civil war-ravaged Syria, Chancellor (now former) Angela Merkel welcomed many of them.

Britain made the same mistake after World War II when it needed cheaper labour. There were ready arrivals from the West Indies, India and Pakistan. Now there are problems with civic living in this multi-racial national life. In the 17th and the 18th centuries, the USA imported slaves from West Africa on a large scale. As we have noted, there was a four-year Civil War between the northern states who wanted to abolish slavery and the southern ones, who saw this evil and inhuman institution as their legitimate way of life. But the American leadership did not learn their lesson and freely allowed in more and more other settlers. The Democratic Party supports them whereas the Republicans wish to largely retain the white (European) character of the USA. Hence, the Blue versus Red states divergence referred to above.

Who is India to give advice to these countries? It has also blundered. At Partition time and throughout 1946-47, the Muslim League insisted on an exchange of population as the homeland called Pakistan was for all the Islamic people of the subcontinent. Dr. Rajendra Prasad, India's first President wrote a book on the subject called *India Divided*, offering an answer for those who could not move out. They could stay on, but not as citizens. Instead, they would be treated as aliens with residence visas, sans political rights. Pakistan's founder Mohammad Ali Jinnah endorsed Dr. Prasad's views. But Gandhi and Jawaharlal Nehru not only opposed this practical solution, but were unjust to millions of people. The distinguished Pakistani scholar Ayesha Jalal in her book *The Sole Spokesman* has raised the question: why Partition then? The Muslim-majority provinces like Punjab and Bengal did not need nor want the break; it were mainly the Muslim-minority provinces like UP and Bombay Presidency which pressed for it. Eventually, their minorities largely got left behind in India. What a fiasco it has turned out to be?

* * *

35. THE NEED TO INDIANIZE THE JUDICIARY

The Home Minister of India has reportedly addressed a letter to the Chief Justices of the upper courts as well as parliamentary lawmakers to make a "people-centric legal structure". This is overdue across the country. Litigants in many cases do not understand judges' orders, except through their advocates. One reason is that those litigating do not all know sufficient English to be able to read their petitions/ affidavits nor do they understand judges' orders when delivered.

Coming down from the Supreme and the High Courts to the lower judicial arenas, the difficulties increase due to language. One advantage is that clients are nearer the judges and the English spoken is simpler. The first step that needs to be the taken across the country for making the judiciary people-centric is to insist that the language of litigation, up to the district level, should be the local one. If necessary, law books should be printed in two languages, the local lingo and English to help the odd judge or pleader who may have studied in an English-medium school. The pleading as well as what the judges say should also be in the local language.

We know that Law Commission has edited the statute books and deleted many an obsolete law. This is desirable, but does not Indianize Indian law; it shortens the list of laws and must therefore be welcomed. The attempt now should be to cut out those laws that are contrary to the Indian ethos. The current laws contain a great deal originating from Roman law.

The Indian Penal Code was given specifically to us by British scholars like Lord Roger John Laugharne and Thomas Babington Macaulay less than two centuries ago. The latter's Penal Code is an admirable piece of drafting but often is in contravention of the Indian ethos.

Take for example, Section 309, which applies to suicide. It is a crime under Macaulay's prescription; although the Hindu universe permits it for a noble cause like the pursuit of attaining early *mukti* (salvation). The Indian Penal Code has no window of exemption from such an act in pursuit of salvation. Lately, though, some European countries like the Netherlands and Switzerland officially permit euthanasia for several reasons, such as suffering from a terminal illness.

Hindus and Buddhists are permitted to undergo *samadhi* or voluntarily shedding one's body through austere yogic practice. The intention is to avoid rebirth or achieve nirvana. The Jains believe in the sanctity of *santharo* or cessation of consuming food and water until the soul leaves the body. The objective is to attain *moksha* or release from rebirth. The ethos is driven by laws that innate from dharma, not any jurisprudence.

This is not to suggest that all or most laws must be changed or amended; if we were to do so, we could fall out of the mainstream jurisprudence practiced internationally. From this point of view, we are fortunate that our laws are similar to those practiced in the West. Unlike us, the Chinese are caught in a trap; most countries are unfamiliar with conventions and practices China's mandarins prescribed as laws. For inviting foreign investors, the mandarins have to make rules that foreigners can empathize with and also do not violate the mandarin worldview.

There are other factors that contradict not only Indian ethos but also the Constitution, as well as any principle of consistency; marriage, for instance. Article 14 guarantees equality to all citizens before law. A Muslim man can marry up to four wives at any given time but his wife cannot have more than one husband. The two are assumed to belong to an identical community but this is nothing but discrimination by gender. All such irregularities need to be eliminated. Also, what is needed a simplification of the language whose translations in the local tongues should be readily available.

In ancient India, when the indigenous laws based on dharma were practiced, the procedures were simple. The proceedings were informal and more in the nature of mediation, not arbitration or litigation. There were no formal lawyers; some priest-like gentleman would help out if the petitioners and respondents could not articulate their viewpoints. A representative of the ruler helped to conduct the mediation and mostly brought about an agreement between the parties; if not, then often a compromise was ordered. There were no adjournments; if either party did not feel satisfied with the mediation or its resulting comprise, an appeal was heard on a day convenient to the minister or official in the charge of legal affairs and generally, his verdict was final. Only issues of life and death were heard by the ruler, whose verdict was final.

Such procedure survived the conquest of parts of India by Islamic rulers. The change came about when the shadow of Shariat fell upon rules and laws based on dharma. The second drastic change was the replacement in many of the courts by the language used. Persian became the court lingo in most courts. This continued until the East India Company and after the Crown takeover of India in 1858, when the local languages were introduced in the lower courts and English in the higher ones.

Chief Justice of India N. V. Ramana has recently called for the Indianization of the country's legal system pointing out that the colonial rules currently followed may not be suited to the needs of the Indian population. The CJI too opines that Indianization of the judiciary means the localization of the justice delivery system.

Justice S. Abdul Nazeer of the Supreme Court in his recent comments on the Indian judicial system has spoken of the need to Indianize the system, which is still riddled with colonial baggage. Justice Nazeer has also referred to the ancient judicial system in India that demanded justice even from kings. His critique of the current Indian legal system is on account of its colonial psyche while administering justice, which demanded a surrender of rights to the rulers, and granting justice as a matter of privilege and not right.

* * *

36. WHAT IS HAPPENING IN KAZAKHSTAN?

Soldiers shot at protesters in Kazakhstan's biggest city Almaty on January 6th this year, after a few days of violent unrest. The riots have prompted the ruling regime to declare a state of emergency and appeal for help from its ally Russia and other ex-Soviet republics, all of which were once part of the now deceased Soviet Union. Dozens of people have died in the riots and thousands have been detained in this Central Asian country over the past week during the worst violence seen in the country since it became independent in the early 1990s, following the breakup of the Soviet Union. Security forces seem to have reclaimed the streets of the country's main city a day after Russian paratroopers arrived to help quash the uprising.

Kazakhstan is located between Russia and China and also shares borders with three other ex-Soviet republics. It is the largest economy in Central Asia, with rich hydrocarbon and metal deposits. Kazakhstan is the top global producer of uranium and world's second largest miner of bitcoin after The United States of America. It has attracted hundreds of billions of dollars in foreign investment since becoming independent in 1991.

Kazakhstan is the top global producer of uranium and the recent unrest has caused an 8 percent jump in the price of the metal that fuels nuclear power plants. It is the world's ninth biggest oil exporter, producing some 85.7 million tonnes in 2021, and its 10th largest producer of coal.

For a petroleum-rich country such as Kazakhstan to have to raise, or rather double, price of the fuel in one go is surprising. However, the Soviet leaders turned non-communist did not have a reputation of efficient governance. The common folk believed that the leaders are corrupt, whether they are or not is not out in the open. The present prime minister Kassym-Jomart Tokayev is new, having taken over recent from the 81 year old Nursultan Nazarbayev, and yet to prove himself.

For Russia, Kazakhstan is of vital importance since the Baikonur Cosmodrome is Moscow's sole lunching paid for manned space missions. There is none on the Russian end and therefore, it cannot let Baikonur go into alien hands. On the other hand, President Putin's government is busy on the Ukrainian front, having deployed a large military force on its south-eastern border. It is therefore not the best time for Russia to go and intervene in Kazakhstan. At the same time, Chinese President Xi Jinping has conveyed to Prime Minister Tokayev to ensure that his government's action on the people should be highly responsible. China and Kazakhstan share a border.

The yellow giant is a land-hungry country while Kazakhstan is one of the world's largest countries in terms of land area with only about 6 persons per square kilometre. Kazakhstan has therefore to be cautious in what its government does, how sternly or gently it treats its currently rebellions citizens. For the present, the law and order is being helped by the presence of some 3,000 odd soldiers that Moscow has urgently sent. They are on the streets armed with orders to shoot to kill. Several hundred agitating Kazakhs have already been killed and many more injured in firing.

The picture is incomplete if we do not take note of U.S. Foreign Secretary Antony Blinken's diplomatic moves, who has two days ago said that the President Biden's administration is very concerned about the situation in Kazakhstan. Blinken iterated Washington's full support for Kazakhstan's constitutional institutions and also stressed on the importance of respecting human rights, media freedom et al. Evidently, there are more cooks ready to dabble in the Kazakh kitchen than there is meat to cook in there. What America can, or wishes to do in this faraway Central Asian country is a matter of wonder.

Two more points have been talked about in the media. One is that if people on the streets of Almaty see Russian soldiers, they would react strongly. And if the Russians see on television their soldiers on the streets of Almaty being killed by Kazakh rebel bullets, they would react furiously. No one except those in charge in Moscow and Almaty seems to know what exactly is happening on the streets of Kazakhstan. One can only guess that political opponents of the Tokayev regime have seized this opportune time to try and overturn the government. Are they political autocrats or democrats, it is difficult to tell because we do not know them. The government for its part has described them as bandits or terrorists.

However, one factor is certain and that is that history is against autocracy. Information and the spread of knowledge have by now reached mindboggling dimensions and levels. What with the Information Technology, the Google, the YouTube, the versatile mobile telephony and super-smart phones, e-mail and what not, it is difficult to not know. Very recently, one heard on TV that one out of two adults on earth have a mobile telephone. Evidently, facts are known immediately, almost in a flash, though not necessarily the explanations beyond the facts.

A hundred years ago, few would have debated as to which is better, autocracy or democracy. Many considered a benevolent dictator to be an ideal compromise. That is not certainly the case anymore, with the information being the catalyst.

* * *

37. TIRUMURTI'S STATEMENT AT UN

There is no doubt that the Hindus have had an image of being soft and therefore a useful punching bag. It was overdue for a firm stand to be taken as was rightly done by TS Tirumurti, the Indian permanent representative to the United Nations very recently. Swami Vivekananda was palpably aware of the Hindu image having been tarnished and there is a Hindu phobia. While extending the Swami a tumultuous welcome on his return from overseas after making a great name for himself and his faith overseas, Swamiji gave a frank explanation for why there was Hindu phobia.

Sir Sankaran Nair, a member of Viceroy's Council, in his book called *Gandhi and Anarchy* published by Tagore & Company, Madras, 1922, wrote 'for sheer brutality on women, I do not remember anything in history to match the Malabar rebellion. It broke out about the 20th of August (1921). Even by the 6th of September the results were dreadful.'

Gandhiji's comment which he wrote in Young India of 29th September, 1921: 'We have forgotten the divine out of dying for our faiths without retaliation… The Hindus must have the courage and the faith to feel that they can protect their religion in spite of such fanatical eruptions.' He warned the government against excessive repression of the Moplahs. The ending of the revolt was a matter not only of urgency, but of simple humanity: 'Be the Moplahs be ever so bad, they deserve to be treated as human beings.'

Amongst Swami Dayanand' successors, Swami Shraddhananda was the most successful in implementing *shuddhi*. He was murdered in his sick-bed. Gandhi's comment was 'I have called Abdul Rashid a brother and I repeat it. I do not even regard him as guilty of Swami's murder. Guilty indeed are those who excited feeling of hatred against one and another.'

The message of Vivekananda was clear that many problems have their roots in ourselves. There is no power in the universe to injure us unless we first injure ourselves. One-fifth of the population of India has become Mohammedan. Whose fault is it? One of our historians says in ever-memorable language: 'Why should these poor wretches starve and die of thirst when the perennial fountain of life is flowing by? The question is: What did we do for these people who forsook their own religion? Why should they have become Mohammedan?'

To go back to Aurangzeb, over two centuries after the desecration, F. Growse felt that the Magistrate of the district in the 1870s: of all the sacred places in India, none enjoys a greater popularity than the capital of Braj, the holy city of Mathura. For nine months in the year, festival follows upon festival in rapid succession and the ghats and temples are daily thronged with new troops of way-worn pilgrims. So great is the sanctity of the spot that its panegyrists do not hesitate to declare that a single day spent at Mathura is more meritorious than a lifetime passed at Benares. All this celebrity is due to the fact of it being the birthplace of the Krishna.

In his Mathura: A District Memoir, Growse, has recorded his exhaustive survey of Brajbhoomi. He was so overhelmed by the vandalism that visited the area repeatedly, that he wrote feelingly, although his home was in far away England. To quote: 'thanks to Muhammadan intolerance, there is not a single building if any antiquity either in the city itself or its environs. Its most famous temple — that dedicated to Kesava Deva (Krishna) — was destroyed in 1669, the eleventh year of the reign of the iconoclast Aurangzeb. The mosque (idgah) erected on its ruins is a building of little architectural value?'

Today, Balkrishna is worshipped in a little room which appears like a servant quarter adjoining the back of the idgah. Pathos can be experienced by any visitor, whether a devotee or otherwise.

The mischief with masjid extends from Somnath in the west to Adina mosque on the Bangladesh border in the east. The Adina mosque is situated on National Highway No. 34 near Gaur. On the wall outside, distinct remnants of Hindu deities are visible. One stone slab displays Ganesh by the side of his consort. Inside the mosque, the stone work is equally convincing that the original building was a temple.

There has obviously been a fair amount of work done on this place of worship. Memoirs of Gaur and Pandua by M. Abid Ali Khan subsequently revised by H.P. Stapleton prove this.

A more recent work of scholarship is entitled Mosque Architecture of Pre-Mughal Bengal by Dr. Syed Mahmudul Hasan. Evidently, local legend as to who built the Adina mosque and why, appears to be incorrect. According to scholars, it was established by Sultan Sikandar Shah between 1366 and 1374 AD. There is a difference of opinion especially between J.H. Ravenshaw and other scholars as to whether Gaur, the famous capital of medieval Bengal was older or whether Hazrat Pandua, where Adina is located, flourished earlier. The significance of the controversy is about how much rubble from pre-Islamic edifices could have been used. Dr. Hasan is impartial enough to quote various scholars at length, although he betrays some unhappiness at the allegation about use of Hindu material.

* * *

38. NETAJI WON FREEDOM FINALLY, NOT CONGRESS

A conversation took place between former British Prime Minister Clement Attlee and the then acting Governor of West Bengal Justice PB Chakraborthy. In 1956; Clement Attlee had come to India and stayed as a guest of the then governor. Remember, Attlee was the man, who as British Prime Minister had signed on the decision to grant Independence to India.

Chakraborthy then wrote a letter to the publisher of R.C. Majumdar's book, A History of Bengal. In this letter, the Chief Justice wrote, 'When I was acting Governor, Lord Attlee, who had given us independence by withdrawing British rule from India, spent two days in the Governor's palace during his tour of India. At that time, I had a prolonged discussion with him regarding the real factors that had led the British to quit India.'

Chakraborthy adds, 'My direct question to Attlee was that since Gandhi's Quit India movement had tapered off quite some time ago and in 1947 no such new compelling situation had arisen that would necessitate a hasty British departure, why did they had to leave?' 'In his reply, Attlee cited several reasons, the principal among them being the erosion of loyalty to the British crown among the Indian army and Navy personnel as a result of the military activities of Netaji,' Justice Chakraborthy says.

That's not all. Chakraborthy adds, 'Toward the end of our discussion I asked Attlee what was the extent of Gandhi's influence upon the British decision to quit India. Hearing this question, Attlee's lips became twisted in a sarcastic smile as he slowly chewed out the word, m-i-n-i-m-a-l!'

This startling conversation was first published by the Institute of Historical Review by author Ranjan Borra in 1982, in his piece on Netaji's, the Indian National Army and the war of India's liberation. To understand the significance of Attlee's assertion, we have to go back in time to 1945. The Second World War had ended. The allied powers led by Britain and the United States, had won. The axis powers led by Hitler's Germany had been vanquished. The victors wanted to impose justice on the defeated armies. In India, officers of Netaji Bose's Indian National Army was put on trial for treason, torture, murder. This series of court martials, came to be known as the Red Fort trials.

Indians serving in the British armed forces were inflamed by the Red Fort trials. In February 1946, almost 20,000 sailors of the Royal Indian Navy serving on 78 ships mutinied against the Empire. They went around Mumbai and Karachi with portraits of Netaji and forced the British to shout Jai Hind and other INA slogans. The rebels brought down the Union Jack on their ships and refused to obey their British masters. This mutiny was followed by similar rebellions in the Royal Indian Air Force and also in the British Indian Army units in Jabalpur. The British were terrified. After the Second World War, 2.5 million Indian soldiers were being de-commissioned from the British Army. Military intelligence reports in 1946 indicated that the Indian soldiers were inflamed and could not be relied upon to obey their British officers. There were only 40,000 British troops in India at the time. Most were eager to go home and in no mood to fight the 2.5 million battle hardened Indian soldiers who were being demobilized. It is under these circumstances that the British decided to grant independence to India.

The idea is not to in any way undermine the significant contribution of Mahatma Gandhi or Pandit Nehru in awakening the masses to the value of freedom. But to spark a debate about the real contribution of Netaji Subhas and the role played by him and the Indian National Army. School textbooks are dominated by the role played by the non-violent movement. While the role of the INA is dismissed in a few cursory paragraphs. The time has come to revisit modern Indian history and acknowledge the immense contribution of Netaji in helping India win its freedom.

Bose was so popular as Congress President in 1938 that the members made him contest again in 1939. Gandhiji did not approve of the re-election and, in due course squeezed out of the young leader from the Party. In 1940, Netaji was put under home arrest in Calcutta from where he decided to abscond in order to join Germany which was fighting World War II against Britain. The land route was difficult with several visas required on the way. After a hard struggle, Netaji reached Berlin in April 1941 or three months after leaving Calcutta.

After the Japanese declared war on America and UK Hitler suggested that Netaji could do be more useful against the British. He, therefore, agreed to proceed across half the globe by submarine. He reached Singapore en route to Tokyo by the middle of 1943, soon to take over an incipient Indian National Army founded by the patriot by the Rash Behari Ghosh. From a motley crowd of less than 10,000, Netaji within weeks built the army into 50,000 soldiers disciplined forces, by persuading British Indian POWs, that fought until the end of the war. Tragically, it took Bose's life in an accidental air-crash. India's brightest lamp of patriotism was blown out.

* * *

39. JUDICIARY AND INDEPENDENCE

Chief Justice N.V. Ramana has recently said that common litigants are guided by resource and energy sapping litigations need quick justice. He had earlier said that the inadequately supported judiciary costs the country foreign investments and therefore, economic growth. He has implored the central government to ensure financial autonomy for his institution. Such reforms would bring about different results, including improving the GDP and the general growth of the economy.

In the eyes of the common folk, the greatest judicial problem of India has delayed justice and the accumulation of an enormous backlog of cases. If Chief Justice Ramana can show a way of how a person of his stature can suggest ways and means of solving this gigantic problem, it would be better. If some success is met with in this direction, the country as well as the government would be sympathetic.

For a common litigant, it is a matter of great surprise as to why the courts grant adjournments freely. As he/she sees it, that are penalized because most lawyers mark their fees even for the few seconds the adjournment is discussed. What is necessary is to make the asking them to pay half the original court fee for every adjournment. This should therefore bring about another benefit that a busy lawyer can be avoided by a sensible client. He would select somebody to be his advocate who does not have to attend many cases, as well as in several courts in the country.

Another belief of a common litigant would be that appeals should be confined to a maximum of two courts above, preferably one. I have heard that tenancy cases that began in Mumbai's Small Causes Court eventually end up in the Supreme Court. Yet another thought would be, before commencing a final hearing, the judges should ask both sides how much time they would take; say thirty minutes each. If one of the advocates exceeds the thirty minute limit, be it so. But he must pay the cost for every extra minute he continues to argue. These measures should help to distribute cases and litigation to advocates who can efficiently explain their clients problems quickly enough rather than ramble.

We have often called ourselves a poor country, which means fewer assets and more people. If that be so, the same buildings can be used for a second shift. The current procedure is for the High Court to sit for five hours. They can instead begin at 8.30 am and carry on uninterrupted till 1.30 pm and retire for the day. The afternoon session can begin at 2.00 pm and carry on uninterrupted till 7 pm while the judges can be fixed, whether for the morning or afternoon, and change only when the new roster comes out. There is no shortage of lawyers who are prepared to become judges or lawyers who are prepared to appear before them. To test their knowledge before an appointment, there may be an all-India examination to test whether a person is eligible to become a judge or not. The examination can have various levels, depending on the courts where the appointment is to be made.

Yet another problem that plagues India's judicial system is the sheer backlog of cases that have accumulated in its corridors. Similarly, High Courts should also be prescribed the level of litigation they can deal with. This must apply to the lower courts as well. Incidentally, I have come across a Small

Causes partnership case in Saurashtra reaching the apex court. Imagine the number courts and judges the case has to travel!

The other point that must strike the powers that be is that 70 percent of the litigation in India involves various governments. This reflects that a large number of citizens are denied justice unless they try the law courts, which in turn, shows that our laws are not clear and simple, and also open to bureaucratic interpretation with a variety of meanings. I do realize that quite a large number of obsolete laws have been lately scrapped. However, there would be a lot of operating laws that are open to various interpretations. This is the reason for the incidence of voluminous litigation. Clearly, in order to catch up with time, not merely the courts but also the laws would need a change as well as an elimination of the redundant clauses in the various Acts. This would involve the Law Commission.

Another area in which time is wasted is the drafting of petitions and affidavits which are usually long, if not also in out-dated language. As far back as 1976, I had visited London in connection with the purchase of a tea company. The application for sanction to the Reserve Bank of India was drafted by the London lawyer as well as by our Kolkata solicitor. The one written by the overseas lawyer was a page and three lines whereas what came from Kolkata was over six longer pages and a few lines. When I returned to Kolkata, I asked the legal friend whether brevity was the soul of wit. He smiled in embarrassment.

* * *

40. WHY BUDDHADEB REFUSED?

It is a pity that Buddhadeb Bhattacharjee, West Bengal's former chief minister, has refused to accept the Padma Bhushan he was offered on this year's Republic Day by the President of India. The offer was not from the Bharatiya Janata Party government or the Prime Minister. Even his refusal was confused; no one informed him or any member of his family, said Buddhababu, as if that was the reason for declining the honour. The late Jyoti Basu had declined the opportunity of becoming a coalition prime minister when Deve Gowda had to resign as PM. Later, he described his declining as a "historical blunder". The immediate reason given then was his party the CPM, did not permit him to accept the post. While one not might question the genuineness of these persons not accepting either the honour or the executive post, their refusals certainly do say something.

With the demise of Marxism as an ideology the world over, these could be the few opportunities to re-enter the mainstream of politics, in the centre or states. Why not seize them like floral bouquets? Is there something inherently different about communists? It is true that in Eastern Europe, some of them have managed to creep into the mainstream. However, in Europe, politics has swung towards the Right, especially because of a wave of migrants from Africa and Arabia, more so from Syria. In India, the Left is vacant without any prejudicial obstruction as in Europe. In fact, in our country there has been increasing space for politicians of quality; the Congress continues its decline, which is increasingly looks terminal, while no replacement for it as a national opposition has come up. The communists cannot, it appears, see this widening gap.

Is this because the communists are essentially trade union leaders and not politicians? When their trade unions weaken, they sink with their cadres. In the free world, Margaret Thatcher blew the whistle and best the Left could do in Britain as a response to her uncompromising right-wing way of rule was to bring forth Tony Blair, but with the novel label of New Labour, which shunned Leftism during its ten years in power. The Soviet Union collapsed and scattered into 16 republics with the advent of the 1990s. The French and Italian communist parties went virtually out of existence just a little earlier. Nor did Leftism revive in the rest of Europe after 1991. China learnt its lesson from the Soviet Union and converted itself into a pseudo-capitalist system. The Beijing experiment is a novel one with the Communist Party of China owning the armed forces and controlling, with shares, many or most, of China's mega-enterprises. This was done perhaps with the objective of thwarting any revolt against the regime. Citizens there aren't allowed to set up a political party to compete for votes. But isn't this a new version of fascism? Can it last? If so, for how long? After all, the CPC members are not blood relations, and they cannot remain beholden forever. Nevertheless, the Chinese experiment is unique and has been studied by experts, although one must add that this is a work in progress.

Until the 18th century, religion, particularly Christianity provided the governing ideologies through the monarchs. The French Revolution shook up this ideological duality and gave birth to a kind of pseudo-nationalism. To prevent nationalism being used or misused by capitalists, the communists supported by the industrial classes became the antidote to the Soviet Union in the lead. The spectre of communism spreading throughout the continent and engulfing European civilization was very real, and it was in order to prevent such an eventuality that fascism was born. It first came into being in Italy under Benito Mussolini and was soon adopted by Adolf Hitler in Germany, with all its consequences, particularly WWII. Today, both communism and fascism have virtually expired. Some former communists believe that they lost because of their lack of democratic functioning within the party. There can be no denying that parties that spawned and brought this ideology to power acquired dictatorial authority over their respective countries. The result was that the leadership of the fascist parties did not obtain any regular feedback nor any authentic information about how the people felt, or where their countries were headed. Thirdly, people in the world outside also did not come to know as to what was happening in a particular communist country. Regimes did not change often; it was only when a revolutionary cataclysm took place that everyone, inside and outside the country, became aware of what had been wrong. By the time they did become aware, they found that it was too late; they were helpless to stem the tide of change and were swept away by it.

It needs no reiteration that communism as an ideology has no future anywhere in the world. Places like China and North Korea have to use the brute power of the state to remain in power. For any political future in free countries, former communists have to jettison their hidebound mindset and embrace a democratic way of functioning, beginning with their own parties. But given the inherent contradiction between democracy and communism, this does not look like materializing.

* * *

41. ON THE IAS

The first step the governments, both the Centre and states, can take to relieve the shortage of IAS and other senior bureaucrats, is obvious. They should forthwith begin by replacing those, who are in non-bureaucratic assignments, with appropriate professional qualifications as well as experience. For example, there would be any number of IAS officers heading public sector projects, particularly in the states. They have no business to be managing business or industries when they applied for and were appointed for governmental administrative work.

When Sardar Patel thought of replacing the Indian Civil Service and the Imperial Police with the IAS and IPS, he had only administration and policing in mind. Business or industrial management were farthest from his mind. Having been a lawyer in Ahmedabad, he understood enough to realize that to do business and managing industries are a different kettle of fish from administering a sub-division, a district or a division. By the time in the 1950s, the public sector was founded and began growing; he was no more on the scene. He had passed away in December, 1950.

I have professionally grown up in business and/or industry and not at all in government service. But through observation, I have realized the difference early enough. That the government has confused the two hit me when I went on a course in 1972 to the Administrative Staff College at Hyderabad. The institution was coaching working business executives in commercial subjects only. Yet the college was called 'Administrative'. Why? Merely because there was a widespread impression was that the two subject areas were the same or at least similar. Even prominent universities and prestigious business management schools call their courses "business administration". Graduates came out as Bachelors of Business Administration or later, as MBA's. I do blame the government; if academicians can err, so can the governments.

Management Science began as a result of the German army headquarters starting to analyze certain aspects of deploying troops and weapons during World War I. For example, they discovered that for each of their soldiers fighting on the front, they had four persons supporting, supplying or nursing him. On the other hand, the corresponding figures of the British army were 1:10; which meant that it cost about two and a half times per fighting soldier were than the German trooper.

The point I am trying to emphasize is that administration and management are separate subjects demanding different training and skills. At certain points, they do need similar treatment. As a possible example, physics and mathematics may crisscross. But at end of the day, they are distinct and different challenges. Administration requires first of all, a socioeconomic understanding of the area under the administrator being dealt with. The officer must be impartial at all times, following the hot stove principle with the people he administers. He should know elementary law, both civil and criminal. He has to be very careful to keep away from making mistakes while taking decisions because a mistake becomes a precedent.

A business-cum-industrial manager should be aware of these virtues but there are others that are more important for being successful in the conduct of his work. He has to be ideally a quick decision maker and a judge of individuals whom he dealt with. He also has to be more often positive and certainly less negative than the administrator who first analyzes why a certain decision should not be taken. If a manager resorts to such a habit, he may find he has little business to do!

India would have earned money through its PSUs or none at all; hopefully some units might have made profits. What should now be done? Before answering this question, let us be clear that the country has millions of traders but comparatively few industrialists. It would be difficult to develop the economy rapidly with what we have. When I say industrialists I mean men and women with capital enough and more importantly also business integrity. One way or the other, the government will have to participate when it comes to large investments. But before the state again plunges into business activity, the administrator/capital conflict must be resolved.

Today, a 24-year-old IAS officer walks into an office as sub-divisional magistrate and is no less than a chief executive (CEO) of a company. From the word go, he has 200 people working under him. He is virtually a modern-day maharaja whose words are the law of the local land. When we consider the fact that this new appointee, whose only qualification to preside over the fate of multi-billion rupee enterprises is successfully clearing an IAS entrance examination, we can understand the real problem.

The state must not directly invest its money, but advance funds to its financial institutions like insurance, banking. They in turn can consider proposals as the IPOs come up, whether by Indian or foreign entrepreneurs. Let these corporations appoint their own managers, directors et al. The institutions may be represented on the Board of Directors and attend meetings as they are held. No administrator should be in charge of any corporation as hitherto; most of them are wedded to procedure and not profit.

* * *

42. NETAJI

Dear Prof. Sugata Bose,

Give West Bengal a chance; especially when a glorious honour is being done to it. The last 74 years since Partition have been years of trial and tribulation. When in September 1945, our train streamed across the borders of united Bengal, we had arrived in *Sonar Bangla*. The streets of Calcutta, now Kolkata, were washed with piped water twice a day. Park Street could be mistaken for a pathway in London. Then the Great Calcutta Killing of August 1946 showed now much blood could be spilled in the golden land first on its western side and come 1948, also in the east. I was told that people were Bengalis first and religion took a backseat, but this was not so. Over the years, three-fourths of the minority in the east has had to come away to West Bengal. From India's premier industrial state, Bengal today gropes for the wheels of production to turn.

You have said in *His Majesty's Opponent*, that Habibur Rahman, Netaji's companion on his final journey, fought for Pakistan in the Kashmir war. The Prime Minister then was Netaji's chosen elder brother and a left liberal, Jawaharlal Nehru. Should you not cancel your disapproval to Karan Thapar about the Right honouring Subhas Babu? If we do not confuse the future of ten crore people with ideology, a lot of India will come to support West Bengal to rebuild its economy. A great many people, even of West Bengal believe that it was the Left which converted its garden of industry to a graveyard. I have been an active witness to this conversion. It can revive to its pristine glory; I will hasten to claim that the people of Bengal are as skillful as any.

Even at Independence, Bengal was more an agrarian economy than an industrial one. Nearly all the industries had been set up either by the British or a few Indian entrepreneurs, but all from outside the province. Bengalis were either saints like Sri Ramakrishna, Aurobindo, Vivekananda or intellectual reformers like Vidyasagar, Michael Madhusudan or leaders like Banerjee or Surendra Nath Pal, or excellent clerks or farmers. They were not entrepreneurs or even traders. Even sons of zamindars would rather choose trade unionisms' than buy out going concerns sold by the departing industrialists. Yes, Bengalis are also excellent lawyers and doctors like the genius Dr. Bidhan Chandra Roy who could predict from a distance that a person had jaundice coming or bad kidneys. When it came to business, they felt it was the function of *baniks* like the Sahas, Lahas, Dahas et al., who are OBCs in the caste hierarchy. This was unlike northern and western India where banias are considered twice-born and wear the sacred thread.

The Congress did produce upright and competent chief ministers, Dr. Bidhan Roy (same as the doctor), Prafulla Sen, Siddhartha Shankar Ray but economic development was more saintly than political. One CM was so fed up with his United Front Ministry that he sat on a dharma opposite the Writers Building, the Secretariat. Upon a journalist asking him, he retorted, "I am neither a *mukhya mantri* nor a *murkha* (foolish) *mantri*; I am only a *thutho* Jagannath (of Puri)". Jyoti Basu was a gentleman, like any Marxist anti-capitalist but once confessed to me that the state cannot manage industries. Yet his finance minister was Dr. Ashok Mitra, a dye-in-the-wool Marxist, who displayed a portrait of Marx larger than I have seen anywhere. Mitra was recommended to Jyoti Basu on the plea he had been chief economic advisor to Prime Minister Indira Gandhi.

Jyotida's successor was Buddhababu, a refined, educated gentleman who visited China while being chief minister; he came back mightily impressed. He tried to copy China, rather *Sinify* West Bengal without understanding. He overlooked the fact that his was a province of India and not an independent country. He shouldn't have used sale proceeds of land to partly revive the loss making the provincial PSUs. But he is an upright gentleman of a high order, nevertheless.

In the light of these circumstances, the state government should opt to be normal and civil in its behaviour with the Centre. Lately, the policy has been the reverse whether to win elections, score brownie points or regain popularity with the people. However, the times are not the same as in Gopalkrishna Gokhale's days when what Bengal thought, India would think tomorrow. Today, Bengal has a huge debt, its people need to earn more and the state has to develop rapidly.

For the state to develop rapidly, a committee of say, five persons should be appointed, of whom at least three should be with an industrial experience. If a few of the members are from outside the state, so be it. So long as they have imaginative minds which understand Bengal from all viewpoints, it should be fine. Remember, entrepreneurs from outside, whether Indian, or foreign would come to invest in Bengal because they see prospects of profit and not because they are invited.

West Bengal has the potential to bloom as brightly as any flower can. Just quarrel less and smile more, certainly for the supreme honour done to its greatest political son Subhas.

* * *

43. CIVIC VERSUS CULTURAL NATIONALISM

India is being taken over by a "new and imaginary practice of cultural nationalism" as against the "well-established principle of civic nationalism, which seeks to present electoral majority in the guise of a religious majority, and monopolize political power." Thus spoke former Vice-President Hamid Ansari while addressing a conference on protecting constitution. The fact that the former Vice-President chose to make these comments while speaking at an international forum, the Indian American Muslim Council, sharing space with foreign elements some of whom are known to be hostile to the country and its interests, is also not lost on many in this country.

However, the thrust of Hamid Ansari's speech must now bear closer scrutiny. Ansari's allegation is that a civic life has been laid down by the Constitution is sufficient in a pluralistic country. This is far from a welcome assertion. The culture and the history of one community might be distasteful to another. Those not proud of the post-Independence history of theirs because they have stayed back in a Dar-ul-Harb (place of conflict) instead of migrating to their new homeland now prefer their origin to be the Constitution of 1950. This is where there a conflict between culture and civic existence. In the views of a significant segment, the culture of the rest of the country is something that harks back to *jahalia* or darkness.

The former Vice-President's outburst must also therefore, provoke another very serious question, one which the country has so far chosen to put off, but with rather unhealthy outcomes for its body politic. What is so permanent about a country's civic life? The Constitution can be amended; it can be replaced by another document. Our own constitution has been amended more than a hundred times already since 1950, whereas the history of Indian culture would go back to at least the Vedic Age. What probably the former Vice-President referred to was this conflict when he talked of the phenomenon of cultural nationalism seizing power from those who established the principle of civic nationalism possibly operative since 1006 AD and Qutbuddin Aibak or perhaps 1526 AD when Babur won the first Battle of Panipat or any other date.

Those citizens who are desirous of civic nationalism would have to abandon their imaginary preferences and identify with the pristine culture of the country. This, i.e., the partition of the nation was effected in 1947 as Messrs Jinnah, Mohd. Iqbal and Sir Sayyid Ahmad Khan believed in and wanted at any cost. It was a settlement made for all time to come as it appears now. An undoing of that partition means a 60/40 population ratio between the cultural nationalists and the potential civic nation advocates.

Three prominent personalities had envisioned this clash of nationalism; namely, M.A. Jinnah, B.R. Ambedkar and Dr. Rajendra Prasad, our first President. All of them proposed what the League of Nations, the predecessor of the United Nations, had done with respect to Greece and Turkey in 1923. Going back in history, the Turks had conquered the Anatolia and its neighbourhood in the decades preceding 1453. This was the Islamic takeover of legendary Greece. Istanbul was Constantinople until then; the headquarters of the Eastern Christian Church are still situated in this historic city. Through the centuries, there used be clashes between the Turks and the Greeks; in fact, they were rather like what we call communal riots.

The League of Nations, after the end of World War I—when the Turks were amenable to listening after their defeat and collapse of the centuries-old Ottoman Empire—proposed an exchange of Greeks who were to migrate to their original country while all the Turks were to immigrate to Turkey. A detailed procedure of what was to be done, who would do what and by when was documented. The exchange was conducted smoothly and methodically; there has not been a single riot since.

Returning to what former Vice-President Ansari has chosen to articulate, many questions spring to the minds of many concerned countrymen. Why did a former Vice-President choose an international forum to make remarks against the country, whose second-highest office he held for say, ten years? Is there even an iota of merit in Ansari's claim that India is being "torn apart by a new cultural nationalism?" It is also very difficult to ignore the record in public life of country's former vice-president. Also, the fact that Ansari chose the platform of the Indian American Muslim Council (IAMC), a sectarian lobbying group with a long history of anti-India activities, certainly is a poor advocacy for any civic nationalism. Cultural nationalism is nothing but the nation waking up to its fundamental ethos.

The historical track record of this supposed civic nationalism, in promoting tolerance, togetherness, peace and any sense of national security can at best be called a disappointing one. The substance of the former vice-president's remarks, if one were to ignore his diatribe, is also lacking in any specific content as to the exact nature of the threat he has talked about. The country, despite no dearth of serious challenges ever since its independence in 1947, has steadfastly stood by democracy and the very freedom that allowed Hamid Ansari to become the country's Vice-President.

* * *

44. ON HIJAB AND CHOICE

The young college going girls wearing black externals and screaming in protest at the Mahatma Gandhi Memorial College in Udupi district in Karnataka on February 8 had donned *burqas* and not *hijabs*. Comparatively very few women wear *burqas*, except in West Asia. If it were an essential religious practice for those following Islam, most Muslim women in the world would be termed as non-believers in their religion, as laid down by Prophet Mohammad. Advocate Kamat, pleading before Justice Krishna S. Dixit, was evidently confused. A *hijab* is much briefer than a *burqa* and like the latter, is defined as a medium of seclusion. *Burqa* is called a veil of seclusion of women when they are walking 'abroad', which probably meant taking a walk in an unfamiliar place according to the *Dictionary of Islam* (Thomas Patrick Hughes; published by Rupa & Co., 1999).

Be that as it may, the current *hijab* controversy that has erupted from Karnataka has all the makings of a civil confrontation. Students in huge numbers have taken to the streets in Karnataka, with chants of "Jai Shri Ram". Police personnel and authorities are doing their best to pacify them, but the protesting students have raised a valid point. Educational institutions in a supposedly secular country are not places where open display of religiosity should be allowed. If the religious symbols of one bunch of students are to be tolerated in the name of freedom of choice and belief, there can be no grounds for denying the same right to those who demand wearing saffron scarves or *tilaks* on their foreheads. Advocate Kamat has been quick to jump to the defence of the *hijab*-sporting crowd by saying that wearing the garment is an "essential religious practice for those following Islam", but this again seeks to skirt the real issue. First, according to the advocate, do those Muslim women who do not wear a hijab automatically fall into the category of non-followers of the religion? However, more important is another issue. What legal or constitutional right does a state that calls itself secular, have to lay down what the 'essential practices' of any particular religion are or ought to be? This is what those legal luminaries like Kamat who are pleading for the right to wear *hijab* are seeking, in demanding state enforcement of religious obscurantism of some particular community.

Some other states, Madhya Pradesh in particular have been quick to join issue by stating that students are required to follow the dress code laid down in educational institutions, irrespective of the traditions they might be following at home or in their respective private spaces. Madhya Pradesh's education minister Inder Singh Parmar has, in reaction to the Karnataka *hijab* row, advocated a complete ban on *hijab* worn by Muslims in schools in Madhya Pradesh and has stated his government's intent to apply a strict dress code in the state's schools. The minister has also stated that beginning next session, the state government will issue rules and regulations related to uniform dress codes.

Religious, constitutional and legalistic arguments apart, the country's concerned citizens need to play much closer attention to the current *hijab* controversy. The latest row has begun from Karnataka, which is a southern Indian state, where attempts to stoke separatist sentiments have been under way even before India attained its independence from British rule in 1947. Karnataka is also a state that has been witnessing a reassertion of the Hindu identity in recent decades. The ultra-quick reactions by the sections of those who lost power in 2014 is a clear pointer to their involvement to stir up trouble in order to portray the country in a sordid light in the international fora. Shades of a larger conspiracy cannot be missed here.

If *hijab, naqab* and *burqa* are a matter of 'choice', as many of their apologists are claiming on television panels and in columns, the urgency of some girls to wear it now and also make it a matter of political controversy must be questioned. Also, it is likely that the tale will not end here. There will, in most probability, demands raised from certain quarters for permission to perform *namaz* in school and college premises, as these too would arguably comprise "essential religious practices". A backlash in the form of public *pujas* and *aartis* will not take long in manifesting. Next would be demands for "a separate space for performing *namaz*". Would things stop there? Not likely; demands for separate *halal* counters in college canteens, backed by politicians would soon be reverberating. This is not in the domain of imagination, as even the USA and some other Western countries are combating such demands. Further along, demands for time off from class periods for mandatory praying would follow. Given the changed—and changing—political mood in the country, it is not inconceivable that a response from the majority community would soon come forth.

The current row also perhaps demonstrates that it is the apt moment for the country to refocus its attention on the crying need for a uniform civil code, without which all talk of secularism will at best remain a shibboleth. India indeed, remains a unique case of a country that swears by a secularism it refuses to define.

* * *

45. UNIFORM CIVIL CODE

The Allahabad High Court has rightly reminded the government about Article 44 of the Constitution which is a Directive Principle of Policy, which was meant to be parallel to a fundamental right to be implemented in due course. This Article relates to a Uniform Civil Code or a common civil law. It is certainly not to be an imposition of Hindu law on all the communities. Yet, it has not been even drafted for a national discussion. To a lay Indian this appears like a discrimination for two reasons.

All other non-Hindu communities like Christians, Parsees, Jews et al., are happy with the civil law prevailing. Only Muslims are unhappy unless their civil rights under their law called Sharia are allowed to be applied to the civil conduct of Muslims. Essentially, it boils down to marriage and succession rules, especially the former. All other subjects are happily applied to all including Muslims; even the criminal law. Why this discrimination within a discrimination?

Sharia prescribes that if a person is charged for theft, the punishment is to chop off his hand. Muslims do not want this to happen. Possibly because the punishment is too harsh. Is the Indian Penal Code, originally drafted by Lord Macaulay, becomes superior to the Sharia because the former is more convenient? Article 15 of the Constitution begins with the prohibition of discrimination on grounds of religion, race, caste, sex or place of birth.

This Article, an exemplary one, is violated by Muslims themselves. A man is entitled to marry up to four wives but the wives cannot marry more than one husband. A husband can divorce his wife by swearing talaq, talaq, talaq over three months but a wife cannot do the same. For her, there is no talaq; her privilege is confined to *khul* with the help of which a wife can resort to, when the two spouses agree that they have become inimical to each other and their union no longer serves the purpose of marriage, the wife can release herself from the power of her husband by inducing him to separate by paying him a compensation acceptable to him (adapted briefly from the Dictionary of Islam by Thomas Patrick Hughes published in India, Rupa & Co. 1999).

The discrimination continues; where one man is sufficient as a witness, two women are needed. This implies that women is half a human being or a man is a double human. Over and above allowing a man to marry up to four wives, he is allowed to have as many female concubines or domestic slaves as he wishes. A Shia is also allowed temporary marriages which are called *mutah*. These privileges of man and the discrimination woman against may seem unequal or unfair, the conditions of women before the advent of Islam were far worse. The women were extremely degraded in Arabia. They were chattels and an integral part of the estate of a man. Frequent unions between sons-in-law and mothers-in-law were called *Nikahu-al-Maqt* and Prophet Muhammad abolished such hideous practices which were prevailing in old Arabia. In other words; Sharia was a vast improvement on what prevailed before.

At one stage in time, Islam was a progressive religion. As it happened some five centuries after its beginning, *ijtehad* (reinterpretation) by men in power then was stopped. Thereafter, *taqlid* (orthodoxy) has prevailed. Apparently, the men currently in power are handicapped by this injunction. Unless the government intervenes, reform is obviously difficult. In this unfortunate situation, the Muslim women, by today's values and standards, are sinned against.

What to say about the citizens of India who belong other faiths? Their men cannot be called sinned against but certainly they are discriminated against. This is a phenomenon prohibited by Article 15 of the Constitution. Which is greater? The sacred law of a community of citizens? Or the Constitution of the country? Some may argue that the latter is amendable and has been amended some one hundred times. Whereas with the advent of *taqlid* a thousand years ago, Sharia in India has not been reformed. What then is New Delhi to do? Reform and progress or stay put and stagnate? Do not change and discriminate against the kafirs. In the ultimate, it is a choice between *momins* and kafirs and additionally between *momin* women and their men? Therefore, potentially half the momins are for change, justice and progress. The *tarazu* or weighing machine of human justice goes in favour of a Common Civil Code.

The long delay on the part of the government is explained by electoral considerations. In answer to a member's question after passing of the Hindu Code Bill. Nehru told Parliament, "Well, I should like a civil code which applies to everybody but wisdom hinders. If he (the member) or anybody else brings forward a Civil Code Bill, it will have my extreme sympathy. But I confess I do not that at the present moment the time is ripe in India for me to try to push it through. I want to prepare the ground for it".

It was believed, and right so, that Muslims voted solidly at election time, up to 90 percent. The rest of the electorate, in the earlier polls, generally cast only about 40 to 45 percent. The Muslim vote was thus considered twice as effective. Is it may wonder that political parties chased it by pampering it.

* * *

46. THE NEW AVENUE OF EMPLOYMENT

On my first visit to England in 1961, I learnt that Sir Stanley Mathews had retired after playing for several years as a right-back for his club. When young and fully fit, he played in the European Cup but could not participate in the Olympic Games, on the grounds of his being a professional and not an amateur. Cricket too, discriminated against its professionals. They were always referred to by their first names. Fast bowler Harold Larwood, famous or infamous for the Bodyline series of 1932-33 was a professional; his captain, the irascible Jardine, who would enter the pavilion through the gentleman's gate, was an amateur. While Jardine was called D. R. Jardine, Larwood was simply called Harold Larwood.

For years, sport was looked upon as the pastime of gentlemen, who had the means and leisure for it. Sons of groundsmen were recruited by the team or its club to fill empty caps in a team and clubs would pay them for the duration they played. They were called merely players, not gentlemen. Things improved gradually though it looks decades for real change. It is necessary is to recognize mainstream sports as an industry, as well as the activity that goes into the building of the infrastructure. This would ensure money coming into the promotion of sports.

It is sadly surprising that a large country like India hasn't yet fully woken up to the fact that sports are much more than field games. Jagmohan Dalmia of Kolkata could well have been the first entrepreneur to realize the cricket's potential. It was under his leadership of the Cricket Association of Bengal that the Eden Gardens stadium was developed to its current dimension. He raised funds and spent them judiciously. It was Dalmia who empowered the C.A.B. to enable so many youngsters to come up and play cricket, including for India. Further, he obtained for Indian cricket a seat on the high table of the International Cricket Council. This is not a eulogy of an individual but recognition of how someone spotted the potential of cricket and substantially exploited it to the benefit of so many Indians.

Except for this period of time, no one in India appeared to realize that the game is not only for the fitness and pleasure of the players but also a panorama for the entertainment of millions of Indians, like cinema is; except that films began as an arena of performance by comparatively few actors, paid by one, two or three producers for thousands to watch and enjoy for a little money, whereas cricket began as a source of amusement for a few at their own cost on public or acquired land. That non-players began to watch some games was incidental, to begin with, free of charge and in due course with the help of a little payment.

An underdeveloped society should look upon cricket or any sport of mass attraction as an industry. To engage, employ and emolliate lots of people; to play, to coach, to umpire, to build and service the large stadia, to manufacture sports equipment. There would be innumerable avenues of employment as well as earning money. For a country like ours, football, rugby, hockey, kabaddi and many other games could help to expand the sports industry. It should grow into one of the top economic activities, besides improving the health and character of the youth. Before Dalmia, no one appeared to have imagined the enormity of the potential of the ball, bat and stumps.

Orissa's state government has adopted a national hockey team, which is a commendable gesture. Other states should think of football, at one time Bengal's most favourite sport. It began as a virtually cost-free game with no boots and hoses to wear. Even hockey was, at one time, played more barefoot than with boots.

In the 1936 Berlin Olympic Games, Adolf Hitler wanted Germany's hockey team to win the gold medal. The country's national association backed by the government had left no stone unturned to ensure their team's victory. Hitler himself was present at the stadium when the final was played. India's greatest trump card was the legendary Dhyan Chand but at half-time, we were leading by only one-nil which was a wafer thin margin. Maharaja Sayajirao of Baroda was also watching from the stands. As soon as the half time was sounded, the Maharaja rushed to the dressing room to advise Dhyan Chand to discard his boots and switch to barefoot play. He became a different centre forward and scored a total of three goals and India finished the match with a 5-1 win!

After the 1948 Olympics at London, the international rules were changed; for football and hockey, wearing boots became compulsory. Barefoot play became a thing of the past and the games ceased to be artistic and turned more technical. Rules will come and go; change will continue to be the law of life. But sports should grow till it becomes the number one employer of the country. We have many states and Union Territories; there also many games. Let us begin with every state and UT adopt one sport. Before long, India should be a leading light in the Olympics and employer number one at home.

* * *

47. WHY THE JAN SANGH DID NOT TAKE OFF TILL RECENTLY?

A discussion on the central government's performance often evokes a question as why did not the same party do better earlier. Some raise the issue of the partition and ask why did the 1947 polarization not help the Bharatiya Janata Party, or rather its predecessor, not get the electoral advantage then. This is a legitimate question which has not been publically answered as far as I know. The simple explanation is that the Bharatiya Jan Sangh should not have been founded in order to contest the first general election in 1952.

It was in October 1951 that Golwalkar and Dr. Syama Prasad Mookerjee met in a house on Kolkata's then Cornwallis Street. The main agenda was why not start a new party in the shadow of Gandhi's assassination in January 1948 and in the light of the general election scheduled for say March/April 1952. Dr. Mookerjee's proposal was that the RSS should promote a party to which Guruji's reply was that the Sangh was essentially a socio-cultural organization and to bring in politics would disturb its idealistic focus. But if the Doctor, who was already a known political figure, started a party, the RSS would be prepared to nominate two of its tried workers for each province (now state) to set the ball rolling. The Doctor had resigned from the Hindu Mahasabha on the morrow of Gandhiji's assassination nearly three years ago and did not have a large enough team to suffice for an electoral battle as well as the development work thereafter. An agreement was reached between the two Hindu leaders and work began promptly.

To contest a national election, central as well provincial simultaneously, within four months of a party's founding was a tall order. Appropriately from an organizational viewpoint, the Doctor should have returned to the Hindu Mahasabha which was a going set up since 1915, 35 years or more. To ask people, who were not exposed to such an election to vote for a party not heard of, as it were, till yesterday was taking on tough challenge. The Congress was an all–embracing mammoth, moreover there were the socialists called Praja Socialist Party, Dr. Lohia's Socialist Party, the Communist Party et al., Dr. Mookerjee had to offer something distinct; what, if not the Mahasabha? At least, the new party should have been clearly a Hindu platform particularly when the wounds of the partition were still raw. But the word Hindu was deliberately avoided by the leaders; Jan Sangh appeared to be a non-descript name, certainly so in Bengal where our family had settled. I was only 15 years old but this was clearly a feedback my father brought back from his workplace.

Dr. Mookerjee fought from the Rash Bihari Avenue or South Calcutta constituency where we lived; and where his residence was also situated. I saw him campaigning in an open lorry once; he was highly respected and won easily. But only two other Jan Sangh candidates won in the whole country. If he had led the Hindu Mahasabha, the feedback my father got, was that due to the partition, the Nehru Liaquat Pact 1950 to protect minorities and the inflow of refugees then began from East Pakistan, not less than about 40 Lok Sabha seats should have been certain. Remember the Doctor had quit the Nehru cabinet on this very Pact. The influx of refugees from the Punjab, alive, bleeding or dead, had come only until two years earlier but were still unsettled. The absence of the word Hindu in the name of the party and unfamiliarity with the name Jan Sangh took this toll according to the feedback my father collected.

Dr. Mookerjee was a scholar gentleman of the highest order; at the age of 33, he was appointed Vice-Chancellor of the University of Calcutta. Incidentally, his father was Sri Ashutosh Mookerjee and had also been Vice-Chancellor. The Doctor knew the grammar of fair and square play; the rough and tumble of realpolitik was not always his cup of tea. The death of Gandhi, he felt, must be mourned in all its completeness! This in the Doctor's opinion, included quitting the Hindu Mahasabha, of which it was alleged that Gandhi's assassin belonged to it. In Bengal at the time, incidentally, this episode did not arouse the same sympathy it did in the rest of the country. Yet, the Doctor did what was politically not essential. Unfortunately, the name Jana Sangh was akin to a lion in Bengal without his claws.

The party and its member did not have any great legacy of experience. Their interaction with experienced politician came with the formation of the formation of the Janata Party to oppose Indira Gandhi and her Emergency. After its members were forced out from the Janata Party in early 1980, the graduation of the Jana Sangh had begun. Even then, the new ideology they embraced called "Gandhian Socialism" was an act of amateurism, a mixture of two unmixable. The maturity of their political education was achieved only after 2013, when the campaign for the 2014 Lok Sabha elections began. One prominent reason why the Bharatiya Janata Party is learning fast and connecting with masses spontaneously is because its ideology stems from the soil of India. It fact, it is difficult to think of another political thought process in Asia. The party's other two virtues are forward thinking flexibility and absence of rigidity, something that hobbled Soviet Communism.

* * *

48. GOA AND UNIFORM CIVIL CODE

Goa is the only state in India that has uniform civil code regardless of religion, gender, or caste. Goa has a common family law. Thus, Goa is the only Indian state that has a uniform civil code. In Goa Hindu, Muslim, Christians all are bound with the same law related to marriage, divorce, succession. When Goa became a Union Territory in 1961 by the virtue of the Goa Daman and Diu Administration Act 1962, India's parliament authorized the Portuguese civil code of 1867 to Goa which can be amended and repealed by the competent legislature.

In Goa, a marriage is a contract between two people of different sex with the purpose of living together and constituting a legitimate family, which is registered before the office of civil registrar. The particular rules and regulation have to be followed by the parties before they can live together and begin their married life. However, there are certain restrictions according to which these categories of person are prohibited to perform marriage for example: any spouse convicted of committing or abetting the murder of other spouse shall not marry.

Goa is the only state where a uniform civil code is followed. After India annexed Goa in the year 1961, the existing Portuguese Civil Code, 1867 was not altered. It applies to all the Goans living in the state irrespective of their religion. This is an exception, as no other state has adopted a common civil code.

The uniform civil code in Goa is a progressive law that allows equal division of income and property regardless of gender between husband and wife and also between children. Every birth, death and marriage has to be compulsorily registered.

For divorce there are severe provisions. Muslims that have their marriages registered in Goa cannot take more than one wife or divorce by pronouncing "talaq" thrice. During the course of marriage all the property and wealth owned or acquired by each spouse is commonly held by the couple. Each spouse in case of divorce is entitled to a half share of the property and if one dies, the ownership over half of the property is retained by the other.

According to the Uniform Civil Code even if the children (both male and female) have got married and left the house, the other half has to be divided equally among them. Thus the parents cannot disinherit the children totally as they can dispose only half of the property in a will and the rest has to be compulsorily and equally shared amongst the children.

The Goa civil code is largely based on the Portuguese Civil Code (*Código Civil Português*) of 1867, which was introduced in Goa in 1870. Later, the code saw some modifications, based on the Portuguese Gentile Hindu Usages Decrees of 1880 (*Código de usos e costumes dos hindus gentios de Goa*), the Portuguese Decrees on Canonical Marriages of 1946 (*Decreto 35.461: regula o casamento nas colónias portuguesas*) and the Portuguese Decrees on Marriage and Divorce of 1910 (*Lei do Divórcio: Decreto de 3 de Novembro de 1910*). After the establishment of the First Portuguese Republic, the civil code was liberalized to give women more freedom.

The civil code was retained in Goa after its merger with the Indian Union in 1961, although in Portugal, the original Code was replaced by the new Portuguese Civil Code of 1966. In 1981, the Government of India appointed a Personal Law Committee to determine if the non-uniform laws of the Union could be extended to Goa. The Goa Muslim Shariah Organization supported the move, but it was met with stiff resistance from the Muslim Youth Welfare Association and the Goa Muslim Women's Associations.

There are some significant ways in which the Goa Civil Code is different from other Indian laws. A married couple jointly holds ownership of all the assets owned (before the marriage) or acquired (after the marriage) by each spouse. In case of a divorce, each spouse is entitled to a half share of the assets. However, the law also allows antenuptial agreements, which may state a different division of assets in case of a divorce. These agreements also allow the spouses to hold the assets acquired before marriage separately. Such agreements cannot be changed or revoked. A married person cannot sell the property without the consent of his/her spouse.

The parents cannot disinherit their children entirely. At least half of their property has to be passed on to the children compulsorily. This inherited property must be shared equally among the children. Muslim men, who have their marriages registered in Goa, cannot practice polygamy. Also, there is no provision for a verbal divorce.

The Goa Civil Code is not strictly a uniform civil code, as it has specific provisions for certain communities. For example, Hindu men have the right to bigamy under specific circumstances mentioned in *Codes of Usages and Customs of Gentile Hindus of Goa* (if the wife fails to deliver a child by the age of 25, or if she fails to deliver a male child by the age of 30). For other communities, the law prohibits bigamy.

Roman Catholics can solemnize their marriages in church after obtaining a No Objection Certificate from the Civil Registrar. For others, only a civil registration of the marriage is accepted as a proof of marriage. Catholics marrying in the church are excluded from divorce provisions under the civil law. For Hindus, divorce is permitted only on the grounds of adultery by the wife. The law has inequalities in case of adopted and illegitimate children.

* * *

49. REVOLUTION IN INDIA

Lately there is a tendency for the media to debate, discuss, review books and hold interviews on subjects close to the Hindu ideology. But not everyone appears to realize the mega-trend leading them to no longer talk of socialism, Marxism or other relative topics like Revolution and Socialism. These discussions would be nearer solid ground if only the debaters were to accept that we are in the minds of a revolution, whereby India is at least returning to its roots.

Until recently, Indians were confused as if at sea without knowing how to swim. When Independence came, it seemed at last that we had a Pandit, namely, Nehru as Prime Minister but soon enough he told some that he was the last Englishman to rule India. He further said that he was culturally a Muslim and showed his old wedding invitation card which was printed in Urdu. He also proudly declared that he was a Hindu by "accident of birth". He was equally proud to claim that he was a socialist and not long after made the Congress adhere to a policy of establishing a socialistic pattern of society in India.

What was the simple Indian to make out of this maize of claims, mostly alien? Karl Marx defined socialism as 'from each according to his ability to each to according his opportunity'. For the Indian grounded in his faith in karma, it was not easy to swallow that he would have a 'right' to equal opportunity. How could that be when his karma might have been anywhere from excellent, down to the criminal? Thus India's government spoke one language while its citizens understood quite another. Another disconnect that across was in the Lathi town in Amreli district of Gujarat in the late 1960's. The local Member of Parliament was proudly explaining to a few local Congressmen as to how kind and considerate the Nehru government was. There was income tax on rich people going up to 65 percent while the poor were not taxed at all. One worker reacted: "If the rich are taxed high, how does benefit me? My pocket is empty and I cannot afford to pay in any case".

During the same visit at Dhari town, the M.P. told his fellows workers how Tata and Birla were controlled and not allowed to get richer. The local reaction was: "That is why the whole Amreli district had no industry set up by these big industrialists. We have to survive by growing *bajra*. The Nehru government kept the Communist Party pleased; when Indira Gandhi in 1969 split the Congress, the Communists helped to keep her minority government in power. That however did not win the poor man's sympathy. Her nationalization of the coal mines and the big banks thrilled those who could directly make money from them. For the people, it was her charisma and the weakness of the Opposition that kept her Congress in power. For example, the upper and middle class often remarked": Earlier the capitalist families were wealthy, now Indira Gandhi is a big industrialist and banker. How have we benefited? She has not given us any shares in the local mines or the banks, has she?

The Bharatiya Janata Party, and its growth out of the soil and people of India, is one organization which is indigenous. Its Hinduness is unquestionably native. Dr. Babasaheb Ambedkar said that he did not want to die a Hindu; at the same time he did wish to convert to any religion whose origin was foreign. He must have felt that his people would not have been happy; he therefore, chose to change over to Buddhism. A similar logic should apply to a political party. Mohammed

Ali Jinnah precipitated Partition in 1947 in the hope that with Islam being a clear and compact religion, it would bring happiness to its adherents. But it did not. Possibly because it was inspired and founded in Arabia, a hot, dry, sandy region whereas today's Bangladesh is green and wet, while today's Pakistan is also different.

On the other hand, the Hindu ethos has a unique oneness despite its unusual variety. Between Shiva and Krishna, different outlooks cover all the Hindus of the huge country. This is despite most temples being free and independent, guided by the *mahant* of each. Christians and Muslims think that Hinduism is polytheistic. Yet there is no insistence on the concept of God in the Abrahamic faiths. Even an agnostic is acceptable as a Hindu. The ultimate commonality in Hinduism is faith in the karma of each person or soul leading to his fate. Every action has a reaction equal and opposite; as scientific physics.

The democracy has endured spontaneously is a marvel in a country of such variety. The secret of this success of freedom is the Inductive basis of the Hindu faith or the down to up logic. There is no insistence on one God, one Prophet, one Book and then its logic downwards; an up to down or Deductive approach. Hindu assumptions are few and that is its strength. The Western faiths begin strong but can be brittle in the end. Judaism is a united faith but has shrunk in numbers. Christianity has scattered into many denominations which have not held their followers firmly. Whereas Hinduism has gone on despite its history sodden with invasions and invaders settling here. Its endurance has been remarkable, whether politically or in faith.

* * *

50. AMERICA AND ALLIANCES

Speaking on February 26th on CNN, well known American columnist and television personality Fareed Zakaria was pessimistic about the prospects of Ukraine in its current clash against Russia. Zakaria felt that for the next several decades, India would have to face China's hostility. New Delhi should therefore, align itself solidly with the USA. In any case, the Ministry of External Affairs should forget its old habit of dancing with neutralism. Coming from a former Indian, Zakaria's advice must be taken as earnest.

However, it would be advisable to look at America's record as an ally, written, spoken or implicit. Towards the end of World War I, President Woodrow Wilson promoted the establishment of the League of Nations, headquartered at Geneva. Its function was to be similar to that of its successor, the United Nations Organisation. The League functioned to the extent of conducting an exchange of population between Bulgaria and Turkey, as well as Greece and Turkey. Unfortunately, the American Senate based at the Capitol in Washington DC refused to endorse the unnecessary involvement of the USA in Europe's affairs. That, effectively, was the end of the League of Nations, and idea that had been conceived and actively promoted by an American President.

World War II broke out on September 1, 1939, when Germany's Wehrmacht invaded Poland, which had a written treaty of alliance with Britain and France, according to which if any of the three countries were to be attacked, all three would fight together to defend one another. Yet, in September 1939, Britain and France did nothing other than expressing sympathy for Poland, which was overrun in its west by Adolf Hitler and the east by Josef Stalin. Never before had history witnessed horses being butchered by battle tanks, a fate that befell the cavalry units of the Polish army when German Panzer tanks were unleashed on them. So much for the value of an alliance.

The USA is racially an Anglo-Saxon nation. The cultural bonds between the US and Britain are fraternal and close. Prime Minister Winston Churchill's mother Lady Randolph Churchill was an American. After the Battle of Britain, the crucial clash between the air forces of Britain and Germany in the summer of 1940, Churchill realized that there was no way for his country on its own to overcome Nazi Germany. He flew to Washington DC to appeal to President Franklin Roosevelt as well as the US Congress to come to the aid of their British brethren. Else, the fear was that Western civilization would go under the Nazi jackboot. Churchill returned empty-handed, save for an American promise to supply arms on a rental basis, called the Lend Lease. This was despite Churchill's stirring appeal to Washington: "Had my father been an American and not my mother, would you not have helped me?" Such was the 'fraternity' between the two Anglo-Saxon partners.

Washington didn't anticipate that Japan would soon sail across half the Pacific—undetected—and destroy Pearl Harbor, America's vital naval base, on December 7th, 1941. The USA then declared war on Japan, which retaliated with a similar declaration. The Axis alliance of Germany, Italy and Japan required that if any of these countries were at war, the other two would join in immediately. Consequently, Germany and Italy declared war on the USA. It was thus only in

December 1941 that this European conflict, which had begun more than two years ago, truly became a world war, leaving no option for the USA but to join it. In other words, the USA entered the fray only when it was attacked; it did not fight when its brother was desperately in need.

Taiwan, another country that is an American ally and faces an expansionist China, to a considerable extent, is ethnically Chinese, but its leader Chiang Kai Shek was allied to the USA until his defeat at the hands of Mao Zedong in China's civil war that ensued from 1945 to 1949. It was Chiang who led many of his followers to the island that is today Taiwan. The country's political system is democracy, while its economic ideology is free and liberal. Taiwan was not only admitted to the United Nations promptly, but also continued as a member of the Security Council. When the threat of war from mainland China grew graver, a security agreement to protect Taiwan was signed with the USA. That agreement, the Taiwan Relations Act, is still in force, although in 1972, quite casually, Taiwan was removed from the Security Council and its seat was given to Communist China, which is now considered an adversarial nation.

This American habit of engaging in a tango for change is a source of apprehension to potential allies. Fareed Zakaria oblivious of such changes, he cannot be in any position to be advising India's foreign policy moves. In any case, for a large country, it is desirable to be self-reliant and flexible toward the changing tunes of international affairs. The economic benefits that could accrue from a wealthy ally would be too small for a large country, while the USA's willingness to come to the aid of allies in the event of their need is doubtful.

* * *

51. PUTIN, RUSSIA AND TERRITORY

It is surprising that leaders of even big powers live in the long past age of imperialism. What must be the instinct holding them a century or two back, rather than growing up in step with the times today? Before the onset of the Industrial Revolution, understandably, land was the most valuable asset there was. Whether for farming on the surface, fishing around it, or mining below it, any other production, would depend on what the land and water could yield. In those times, if Moscow had craved for territory, as is evident in Ukraine, it would have been understandable. But to lay observers today, the Russia invasion that is afoot appears to be an act of greed, or perhaps the lack of statesmanship.

Russia has no shortage of money, as well as oil and gas. With these assets, guarantees could have been underwritten, whether with the help of Germany or France, or both. Russia could have arrived at an agreement with Ukraine, along the lines of "one, country, and two systems". Moscow could have retained control over defence and diplomacy, leaving culture and economy entirely at the discretion of Kyiv. It is true that Ukraine was part of the former Soviet Union for decades together. The two countries also share historical ties from ancient times. Many Ukrainians speak Russian, especially in the eastern half. Incidentally, the most illustrious successor of Josef Stalin was Nikita Khrushchev, a Ukrainian. Nevertheless, Russian-speaking or otherwise, most Ukrainians would be more attracted by the West European style of living and life, rather than the sombre and joyless Soviet or Russian system.

They could be allowed to enjoy a livelier Western standard of living under a framework of one country with two systems, guaranteed, as mentioned above, with money and third country-underwriting. In any case, Russia has more land than virtually the entire sky, most of which it is still not utilized in an optimal way.

As a Russian sympathizer, my concerns lie elsewhere than the immediate unfolding story of Russia's military operation to its west. More serious concerns loom in the east. I often worry about the future of Siberia and beyond. China, Russia's large and revanchist neighbour, is land hungry. Would it not be looking at Siberia wistfully? In 1969, China actually tried to invade the Soviet Union across the Ussuri River and took away a large number of islands on that river. We can recall how the state of Alaska was sold by the Czar Alexander II of Russia in 1867, to the United States of America, for a sum of 7.2 million dollars. For President Putin's Russia, it is wiser to look East in his fixation about land, rather than focusing on the West, as it is doing now, for the sake of territory.

There is a widespread impression that perhaps President Putin is motivated to recover as much of the territory his predecessor Mikhail Gorbachev had to give up in 1991, as he had to. The unworkable ideology of communism had finally taken its toll on the Soviet Union and caused its collapse. One has to recall that Gorbachev had to allow 15 of the total 16 Republics of the Soviet Union to go free. Given this historical background, and also the fact that Ukraine has tasted freedom and a greater measure of economic development for the past thirty and more years, it is not exactly fair of President Putin to expect Ukraine to return to the Russian Empire. It is this imperial mentality, which we have flagged as obsolete at the beginning of this article, which is the spoiler. At least three responsible Russians had told me in Kolkata, long before 1991 that their country needed to be more cohesive if it is to progress and not decline. At the time, there were three streams of civilization competing in the Soviet Union—Christianity, Islam and Communism—to have their say, as to how the country should move ahead. As these gentlemen saw it, the competing superpower, the USA, which functioned on only one ethos, was a straightforward case.

That territory is no longer as important an economic asset was proved by Germany and Japan in the post-WWII era. Germany, after the defeat of its Nazi regime in 1945, was divided between West and East; two-thirds and one-third respectively until the year 1989. Yet, West Germany took long economic strides and became one of the most prosperous countries of the world. Japan at the end of the war, lost Manchuria, Korea, the Curil and other islands; yet became the world's second biggest economy by the 1980s, plus a technological superpower. The situation was different when Britain, France, the Netherlands, Portugal and Belgium crossed into Asia and Africa to conquer territories in order to develop their own economies. The industries followed thereafter. With the advent of industrial technology and international marketing, unlimited land or territory was not necessary. Before this era, the imperial compulsion was to capture one's neighbour, and if this was not possible, one went overseas. Yet before this era, Portugal and Spain went to South America and Christopher Columbus sailed to the New World, which led to the establishment of the USA.

* * *

52. ARIF REJECTS MAJORITY-MINORITY

Arif Mohammad Khan, currently Governor of Kerala, has given a fulsome interview to the media; which should be a useful guide to many of our citizens. The former Union minister and once a leading Congressman says that anyone who wins an election and comes to power can be called as being in majority and anyone who loses and remains on the opposite side is in the minority. He is opposed to the appointment of minority commissions; he prefers human rights panels in order to cater to the needs of those marginalized or perceiving their fundamental human rights under threat. Viewed from the lens of the fundamental requirement of any country that prides itself on being democratic and secular, the Kerala Governor's logic is irrefutable.

That should bring us to why the label of minority and minorityism came into being, and the subsequent politics around it. Mohammed Ali Jinnah, the founder of Pakistan, agitated for Partition on the plea that Muslims are a nation and not a minority. He argued for his entire nation to emigrate to what some Muslim League leaders called the "New Medina". When he found that not many had migrated, he told the Pakistan Constituent Assembly on August 11, 1947", "You are free to go to your temples, mosques or to any other place or worship in this State of Pakistan. You may belong to any religion or caste or creed—that has nothing to do with the business of the State". However, Jinnah was perhaps too old and sick to enforce the implementation of what he had spoken in August 1947 in the highest Assembly of his new country. As a result, today India has more Muslims than Pakistan!

However, neither Hindus nor Muslims can behave as a separate nation inhabiting the same country. Two nations, aka Jinnah, cannot coexist in one country. Yet some people still continue to behave as if they belong to a separate nation. For the country, the consequences of such recalcitrance are a drag on its progress while for the individuals it is a drag on their future. They and their progeny would indefinitely remain poor and backward; the only beneficiaries could be those who mediate between the poor individuals and God Almighty.

What a piece of news published today in an Indo-Asian News Service survey says is welcome. According to the survey, at least eight percent of the votes cast in the recent Uttar Pradesh elections were reportedly by Muslims in favour of the BJP. Furthermore, the same survey has reported that six of the seats won by the BJP were due to the All-India Majlis-e-Ittehadul Muslimeen (AIMIM) cutting into the community's votes that might otherwise have gone to the Samajwadi Party. AIMIM, a political party based out of Hyderabad, polled nearly 19,000 votes in Firozpur and 2,190 in Sultanpur in the recently concluded elections for the UP Assembly. The other constituencies where AIMIM polled notable votes were Bijnor, Nakur, Kursi and Shahganj where the party had put up its candidates.

If indeed a change of outlook is taking place in UP, it is particularly to be welcomed. Qaid-e-Azam Jinnah had ebulliently described the Aligarh Muslim University (AMU) as "the arsenal of Pakistan". Many of its students spent months canvassing for the Muslim League in Punjab in the 1945-46 election, which ultimately led to Pakistan. When the local the local Punjabis enquired of the campaigners as to what they (meaning the UP Muslims) had to gain from Partition, the latter replied that their campaigning was to "win a New Medina" and to "reinstall a new Khalifa" (Caliph)! From an idealistic point of view, one would indeed grieve at such a mentality, although it is human to err. But it is folly to persist with the error.

Dr. Zakir Hussain, former President of India, once gave sound advice to his Indian co-religionists along with 13 other leaders; he had begun his counsel as long ago as 1951. "Our misguided brothers in Pakistan do not realize that if Muslims in Pakistan can wage a war against Hindus in Kashmir why should not Hindus, sooner or later, retaliate against Muslims in India?"

Another piece of advice subsequently given by him and his friends was "If the Hindus are not welcome in Pakistan, how can we, in all fairness, expect Muslims to be welcomed in India? Such a policy must inevitably, as the past has already shown, result in the uprooting of Muslims in this country and their migration to Pakistan, whereas it became clear last year, they are no longer welcome, lest their influx should destroy Pakistan's economy".

Predictably, the emphatic victory of the BJP in the recently concluded assembly elections, particularly in UP, have set off yet another round of secular wailing and the by now all-too familiar doomsday predictions about the impending doom for secularism, democracy, liberalism and what not. Here again, Kerala Governor Arif Mohammad Khan's worldview, that the idea of a majority-minority divide entrenched in societies today has been sown for the very purpose of creating discontent and hatred, offers the sagest outlook and way ahead. Such binaries derail India's progress. One is a child of India, no matter what the vectors defining us are.

* * *

53. LOOKING BACK AT INDO-RUSSIAN TRADE

For nearly 30 years, Indian producers enjoyed the incidental generosity of the Soviets. "Incidental", because the rouble was valued low. In 1991 the RBI treated the rouble as worth Rs. 18/- whereas it was not worth even 28 paise. The dollar was being auctioned in Moscow at the time for 3000 roubles.

With the collapse of the USSR and the end of the rupee trade, Indian tea exports had declined by one-third. The result was a slump in prices, hopefully to not last long. It should be interesting to pursue this nostalgia further back and recount the highlights of the Indo-Russian trade.

1897 was a year of anxiety in Indian tea exports to Russia. Plague had broken out in the country and import of Indian tea into Batoum, Georgia was therefore prohibited. Initially, the reaction in Calcutta was one of anger and there was some talk of reprisals like stopping the import of kerosene oil pumped in Baku. Calcutta made a timely intervention and persuaded Russians to recognize that tea is no carrier of plague. The crisis was fortunately short-lived. In the year 1903-04, nearly 29,000 pounds of tea were exported from Bombay to Russia. Two years later the quantity had trebled.

About this time, at was discovered that lately there was a strong bias in Russia in favour of land-borne teas and they realized higher prices than their sea-borne counterparts. Nevertheless, the Indo-Russian trade continued to grow. A British report from Odessa said that the Russian tastes had undergone an extraordinary change in the last decade. His preference had swung from China to Indian and Ceylon tea. Purchases from China had declined from by a third.

The consular report went on to add that there had been a steep rise in the demand of green tea between 1904 and 1912, imports had grown by nearly 20 times. The Central Asian provinces had taken to green tea as a kind of substitute for intoxicants which were forbidden by Islam. A whole new market, over and above that of black tea had been created.

When everything was hunky-dory, W.W.I ended and there was a general recession, the crash in tea prices was unprecedented. Between 1919 and 1920 the price for common teas had dropped to one-third. This slump was attributed to the Revolution in Russia. Imports by this consumer had stopped all together.

In due course the Soviet Union resumed imports on a limited scale. A big enough alternate home had not however been found for the surplus tea even a decade later. The annual imports by this country around 1930 ranged around 60 million pounds when contrasted with the prewar figure of 200. Too much was therefore being shipped to Britain causing a continual indigestion there. Trade circles felt that, to save the Industry from ruin, an urgent outlet for up to 100 million pounds had to be found. The Capital of 2 July 1937, reminded that the U.S.S.R was the obvious home for this surplus. And this country was willing to import more provided it was granted long term credit. Apart from relieving the glut, the worry was of generations growing up in Russia without the tea drinking habit.

The Ceylon Association was reported in October 1931 to have turned down the proposal to extend two years of credit to Russia. The reason was that a single Soviet agency bought all the tea. In the event of a default, the loss would be total. Meanwhile, negotiations between the producers and the Soviet government had been going on. The purpose was to ensure continuity of sales of black tea to Russia. The supply was plentiful and the Soviets were keen to buy; the missing link was money. It was at last in July 1934 that a tentative scheme of credit was reported. A trading company was to be formed by the producers of India, Ceylon and the Dutch Indies. The main producers of these countries were to subscribe to the share capital of the company on the basis of £3,750 per million pounds of tea grown. £938 were payable in cash and £2,872 were to cover any default by the Soviets. The joint company was to be known as the Anglo-Russian Tea Trading Company which would buy tea for cash at the auctions in London, Colombo, Calcutta and Amsterdam and sell in Russia on twelve months' credit. Those hopes dashed to the ground when the negotiations were suddenly suspended.

In June 1944, it was reported that the Soviet Union had received more than 35 million pounds of Indian and Ceylon tea through the British Ministry of Food. The trade therefore wondered whether the Russian market might be reopened. The Manchester Guardian expressed tire opinion that there was a bigger opportunity after the war for re-developing the Russian market.

On 12th July, 1948 at New Delhi, the first Indo-Russian food agreement was signed. India would receive 50,000 tons of wheat. In return it would supply 11.5 million pounds or 5,000 metric tons of high grade tea. Some in the trade felt that this would put Indian tea at a disadvantage in the hard currency markets. This conflict between barter and hard currency trade increased as the volume of trade with the Soviet Union went up. In the agreement signed in 1949, 200,000 tons of wheat and 100,000 tons of food grains were to be exchanged for tea, jute and castor oil.

* * *

54. ON HIJAB AND SECULARISM

Without there being consensus or a clarification on what comprises secularism, India as a society and nation will continue to be adrift. The Hijab controversy in Karnataka has also brought to the fore as to what is secularism and how far it should let minorities do what they like. Whether the wearing of hijab extended to ignoring a school uniform and whether it could be extended to all girl classrooms were the questions thrown up.

References to secularism appear often enough in the media. But seldom is a mention made of the Bernard Stasi report which is the latest thesis on what is a secular state. It was submitted in 2003 and was treated as the backgrounder for the secular law which was passed by the French National Assembly in 2004. If defines three essential principles are: freedom of conscience, equality in law for spiritual and religious beliefs, and neutrality of political power.

The report has ordained is that the students attending government schools or employees working in government offices must not display religious symbols of a conspicuous nature which would include even a large cross. There is no restriction on wearing of any form of dress or display of any religious symbols in the country at large. The state, however, has to maintain absolute neutrality between one religion and another. The French insistence on secularism or the absolute separation of the Church from the State goes back to 1905, guaranteeing the free exercise of religious beliefs. The only restrictions were decreed *in the interest of public order.*

The Stasi Report has stated that Islam is believed to be incompatible with secularism. This was the provocation to the investigation carried out of Bernard Stasi and the subsequent passing of the legislation. As far as private employers of schools are concerned, the law is that the will of the institution would prevail and not any idiosyncrasy of the employee. The intention behind the stipulation is to ensure that there is no discrimination against members of any religion. So that an employer does not avoid the appointment of a scarf wearing lady or a skull cap wearing man.

These provisions ensure not only the neutrality of political authority but also the freedom of conscience and belief as well as equality before the law. The Stasi Report has emphasized secularism as a cornerstone of a democracy.

Every state is sovereign and has the right to frame its Constitution as well as its other laws according to the needs of its society. How else has Malaysia declared itself an Islamic Republic completely overlooking the presence of Hindus, Buddhists and Christians who comprise nearly half of the population? Why should Bangladesh and Pakistan have the privilege to call themselves Islamic? Bangladesh had reduced its Hindu population to 10 percent by 1991. The figure for 2001 is awaited. In 1947 Hindus comprised 30 percent of East Bengal. Pakistan has today, according to its own census figures, only one-and-a-half percent Hindus. The rest have suffered ethnic cleansing. The fact that India has never challenged the rights of Bangladesh or Pakistan to do what they have done means that we have respected their sovereignty.

Going further, would the Emirates in West Asia be justified in not allowing a temple to be built on their territory? Should Saudi Arabia have the right to disallow even the entry of a non-Muslim on the soil of Mecca and Madina? Does any universal declaration of human rights apply to these respected members of the international community in general and the UNO in particular? The Stasi report has clarified that Article 9 of the European Convention of Human Rights and Fundamental Freedom does not create an absolute right to religious licence.

Sarva Dharma Sama Bhava does not add up to secularism. The spirit behind these words was universal tolerance. Secularism is essentially the separation of the Church from the state. India never had a big enough Church nor did it ever interfere in the running of the state. Islam on the other hand does not separate the temporal from the spiritual. The ultimate evidence of this was that the Caliph, or the representative of Prophet Mohammed, was the spiritual head and the temporal chief rolled into one. There was no dividing line between the Caeser and God.

In India, the practice during the British Raj was non-interference by the government in affairs of the religion. This was especially so after the so-called Sepoy Mutiny. It was only after Independence and the advent of vote bank politics that *Sarva Dharma Sama Bhava* began to be twisted in order to play one community against the other. Articles 25 to 30 were first introduced in 1946 with the intent of dissuading the Muslim League from insisting on Partition. Mysteriously, however, they survived in the draft Constitution even after the country was torn asunder by Partition. The Marxists also call themselves secular. Their idea, however, is the abolition of religion. Karl Marx had considered religion to be the opium of the masses. In pursuance of his philosophy the Stalinists converted many a church mosque and synagogue into a shop or a museum or an office across the Soviet Union.

* * *

55. WILL BJP REFORGE ITS PROGRAMMES?

Sunday the 20th of March saw an interesting debate in the print media. The point of discussion was whether its resounding victory in the recent Assembly elections would induce the Bharatiya Janata Party to reforge its ideology of governance. The debaters have been anxious to know whether the electoral results were a change of governments or a change of regime. The BJP's ideology of Hinduness has traditionally had a connect with the soil of India. In fact, most other political ideologies the world over are 'isms' based on the socio-economic classes they sprung from, rather than on the specific ethos of the countries concerned. It was so with capitalism, which has had its roots in mercantilism. Socialism and then of course communism which followed it, was conceived of by those who believed that religion is the "opium of the masses" and nationalism is an instrument of the rich exploiting class to keep the toiling working class in chains. In complete contrast to all this, the BJP's ideology and the programmes emanating from it are the nearest to India's own ethos.

The advantage of an ideology that has grown from a country's soil is that the people normally take to it like fish to water. Those who have been influenced by thinking that has originated overseas find it difficult to digest it though. Dr. B.R. Ambedkar (*Complete Works,* published by the Government of Maharashtra) put this point across lucidly. He was at the time thinking of which faith to convert to since he had decided he would not die as a Hindu. His quest led him to reject Islam and

Christianity, because in his words "they would have a denationalizing effect on his people"; those religions have been founded in other countries, namely West Asia. In the end, he chose Buddhism because it was born in India. Has he not proved to be a visionary in the decades since he made his choice some 70 years ago?

Welfarism or a welfare state is one of the themes in vogue in the current milieu, and is supposed to be the touchstone on which the worth of political ideologies ought to be judged. Most students of political science would relate the concept to the West, the term having first emerged in the UK during World War II. It has since been used much more broadly to describe systems of social welfare that have developed since the 19th century. The original promise of a welfare state covered every citizen regardless of income. It offered nothing less than a cradle-to-grave welfare state. That was the great promise dangled before the British electorate in 1945.

But a welfarist society is the traditional concept that has been rooted in India since time immemorial. One need look no farther than the countless *langars* in our gurudwaras and *bhandaras* in temples. Apart from feeding the poor, the meals were donated by those rich or well-to-do willingly. It is therefore a voluntary transfer of wealth from the rich to the needy individual. This is unlike the European method of taxing the rich at high rates. Taxing public money for the supposedly noble purpose of spending the proceeds on the poor is a dubious idea, as no effective mechanism for ensuring the delivery of taxed wealth to its intended beneficiaries has been developed. Regimes and countries that have met with collapse in trying to enforce this system fill the textbooks. Late Prime Minister Rajiv Gandhi had once said that out of every Rs. 100/- allocated for the welfare of the poor, only Rs. 15/- actually reached them. Prime Minister Narendra Modi is acutely aware of this reality and has been insistent on the direct delivery to the intended beneficiaries.

Another Indian reality has been the demand for at least one toilet per family. This need was more acute for orthodox Muslim ladies, who could not expose their faces outside their homes, which would have been inevitable during the daytime. Scholars might reject this point as unnecessary in the context of ideology. We in India question the use of ideology, which does not include every citizen's comfort as essential. Thousands of pages of Marxist and socialist ideology are useful, but ineffective for a leader to make a promise to his electorate.

One particular allegation has been that the BJP polarizes the Indian electorate. Would anybody believe that the party is a club of wastrels, who polarize Hindus and Muslims without rhyme or reason? Yogi Adityanath got only nine votes in one particular pocket in his constituency. In other words, his party is not popular among Muslims everywhere. By polarizing or doing anything against Muslims, the BJP would lose whatever little support it gets from the community, whether men or women. This would apply equally to Mahadalits, or the most backward, among the Hindus.

A new theory is current that traditional electoral democracy has been vitiated by the ruling party to the extent that it is coming in the way of the all-important constitutional democracy. The problem before us is to research what constitutional democracy is, as distinct from electoral. I can only think of the Greek concept of the three classes, of which only the uppermost mattered. I wonder if I am right.

* * *

56. WHAT BIRBHUM REVEALS?

The gruesome killings at Rampurhat in Birbhum district can be seen as another link in the chain of half-sovereignty that has reigned in our country for long. The US declaration of Independence in 1770 was the first document to enunciate sovereignty as an essential element of the new state. The French Constitution of 1791 stated: "Sovereignty is one, indivisible, unalienable and imprescriptibly; it belongs to the nation; no group can attribute sovereignty to itself nor can an individual arrogate it to himself." The concept was first thought of by Jean Bodin of 16th century France to signal the progress from feudalism to nationalism.

Birbhum is not the only district affected by violence. The government recently stated that there still are 40 districts affected by Maoism; in 2005, this stood at over 200 districts. On Independence Day that year the Maoists had killed an Andhra MLA C. Narsi Reddy. Only two weeks earlier, seven persons were butchered in Bastar district of Chhattisgarh; again by Maoists. Leave alone civilians, even the police could not enter sub-divisional towns in the affected areas.

What is happening in West Bengal is not accidental as it has been the policy of the Congress, the Left Front and Trinamool Congress to encourage infiltration, and thus expand their vote-bank. Had it not been so, how would these parties explain their support to the IMDT Act in Assam and being unhappy at its having been struck down as ultra vires by the Supreme Court? Assam was the first state to enact a law of this kind whereby the onus was on the complainant to prove that an immigrant was guilty of having become one through infiltration; not the other way around as in all other states. Such laws cannot survive or even be made law in a sovereign country.

Birbhum has understandably set off a discussion in the print media as to whether the bureaucracy in letting the country down. There is no doubt that the country's bureacracy has substantially become subservient to the ministers. To an extent it is because of human temptation for comfort of work and ease of promotion. There is however, another factor and that is that the bureaucracy's ethos is outdated. From the British era Indian Civil Service, they learned to believe that they are not servants but owners of the country. They however forgot that now the owners are the citizens and not the ministers or their political parties. Moreover, the administrative services bureaucrats began with the belief that they are administrators or enforcers of rules and procedures.

Over the years, recently more so, there has been rising consciousness with regard to development. When people want development, the politicians will hurriedly offer or at least promise *vikas*. This becomes a call to the IAS officers to act like managers who are expected to try and create surpluses from the local economy for material growth. In a way, the officer, now ideally a manager has to move from his focus on procedures to profit or surplus in order to make his district more modern and altogether better. The responsibility for law and order must be shifted entirely to the police service officers, the superintendent and his deputy. With the progress of technology and its machinery, the work of maintaining law or order is easier than before. In fact, all officers IAS, IPS or otherwise would have to reorient their focus. They should all try to bend towards becoming development managers from the erstwhile administrative officers. This is a change from a static vocation to a dynamic approach. The politicians must also change their functioning; they cannot talk of development and behave like old times when connecting with the people and collecting election funds were sufficient.

The bureaucrats are permanent and career-long rulers while the politician is quite frequently a bird that passes after a five year term. The former should take up responsibility for the long-term and reformist aspects of governance. The Congress has always been pro-Muslim. This is clear from the fact that *wakfs* and Muslim personal law still remain untouched collectively, the *wakf* properties represent the biggest urban landlords in India say up to six lakh acres. The demand for Taj Mahal by the UP Sunni Wakf Board and that for Bibi ka Maqbara at Aurangabad by the Maharashtra Wakf Board is baseless as it is on the ground that these contain *qabrs*. A sovereign state should nationalize all its properties.

Similarly, Muslim personal laws still continue to be sacrosanct and above the purview of the Constitution. Contrary to the Supreme Court's view, the Muslim community now appears to have set up Sharia courts known as Darul Qaza in a number of states to adjudicate on matters concerning marriage, divorce, etc. There are, therefore, two systems of law and justice functioning in the country—one Muslim and the other Indian.

The evident conclusion would be that India is a half-sovereign state. This concept was innovated by the German jurist on international law, JJ Moser, who lived in the 18th century. India has some attributes of sovereignty like its belonging to the nation and not to any individual. But between the Sharia and *wakf*, sovereignty is shared and not absolute.

* * *

57. PAKISTAN TODAY

It is difficult, if not impossible, to understand events as they unfold in Pakistan. However, it should not be so for us Indians who have coexisted with Muslims since 1092 AD, or earlier. For quite a large part of this long period, the Muslims ruled large tracts of India. Mughal Emperor Akbar the Great was a genius as a statesman of a good 50-year part of this rule. Not many countries have produced the like of him. What then is the supposed mystery of Pakistan for us?

Pakistan's founder Qaid-e-Azam Jinnah was a brilliant person; for long years, he was the highest paid barrister in the entire British Empire. Pakistan, assuming its merit, was the greatest brief he won. Incidentally, it was a self-given brief and he persuaded the clients—the Muslims of undivided India. Normally, an advocate gets a brief to argue at the behest of client; he does not create one himself. Punjab, Bengal or Sind did not want Pakistan. They were Muslim-majority provinces with Muslim premiers with the whole Indian market at their disposal. Their natural question was—why Partition? The North West Frontier Province was dominated by the Frontier Gandhi, Abdul Ghaffar Khan who was a member of the Congress, which then was against partition. Baluchistan was a separate princely state ruled by the Kalat, and not even part of British India.

Those Muslims keen on a division of India were those who resided in the Muslim minority provinces which willy-nilly were to remain in India. Muslims of UP or United Provinces were the keenest. The Aligarh Muslim University was a stronghold of the Muslim League and an arsenal of Pakistan, in Jinnah's words. They considered it their God-given duty to create a New Medina because the last Caliph of Sunni Islam had been expelled from Istanbul and the institution abolished by Kamal Atatürk. The results of the decisive elections of 1945-46 were a landslide victory for Jinnah.

However, the promised New Medina has not delivered the expected *jannat* to its faithful. In 1971, Pakistan sundered into two, Bangladesh, formerly East Pakistan after a bloody struggle against West Punjabi colonial domination and later genocidal brutality, and the western part which is the current Pakistan, and its defeat by India. The woes of Jinnah's dreamland don't end here. Sind's rallying cry is "Jio Sind" and it wants independence from Pakistan. NWFP or Pakhtunkhwa years for a separate Pathan nation, and has never reconciled to the plainsmen of Punjab. Baluchistan is firm on secession; who wants to remain unites with Punjab-based Pakistan?

Jinnah did not really understand his community the Muslims. Pakistan lacks any quality or even vestige of nationhood, a fundamental fact of history Jinnah had no knowledge of and had no time for, as he was whipping up frenzy among the Muslim masses. Only a single factor—religious identity—can said to be the genesis of Pakistan is driving zeal. Carved out of Hindu-majority India, Pakistan was the culmination of the tussle and conflict between natives who had converted to Islam and the overwhelming who did not. Converts identified with Arab invaders of the last millennium. Shah Waliullah (1703-62), a 'purifier' of Islam on the subcontinent despised local traditions, and pompously declared "We (Indian Muslims) are an Arab people whose fathers have fallen in exile in the country of Hindustan, and

Arabic genealogy and the Arabic language are our pride". Walliullah was worried about the growing power of the Marathas and the Mughals' helplessness against them as Babar's dynasty had begun fading into the twilight of history.

Ironically in the 20th century, it was the impeccably Saville Row-attired, Westernized Jinnah with Victorian manners, a secular enough outlook and an appreciation of finest foods and wines, who articulated the same fears that the 18th century Shah Waliullah had done, although Jinnah was unrecognizably different from Waliullah, a bearded religious scholar. But their arguments were uncannily similar. Jinnah too declared the separateness of Muslims and Hindus, basing his case for Pakistan on the premise that the two peoples could never live together peacefully within one nation state. He nevertheless did articulate the fears and aspirations of an influential section of his co-religionists. The conservative ulema opposed Jinnah and Partition, as they believe that Islam must not be confined to national borders. But Jinnah's argument that Muslims constitute a distinct nation that would be overwhelmed in post-British India by a larger and better-educated Hindu majority won the day.

That being so, why has Pakistan failed to evolve into anything resembling a nation? Its current Prime Minister Imran Khan, another Western-educated playboy and former cricket star, but an army puppet nonetheless, is on his way out, whatever the outcome of the no-confidence vote against him in his country's National Assembly. Imran's failed "Naya Pakistan" might well seed another secession of his country, possibly its dissolution too.

The blame must lie with Jinnah, whose incoherent ideas of what his new country would look like are bearing toxic fruit. A state whose sovereignty rests with Allah and not the people is a medieval theocracy, not a nation. Besides, Pakistan, after its inception, chased the chimera of resurrecting the long-gone Islamic rule over the subcontinent, and not its citizen's welfare, which would merit another article.

* * *

58. SARDAR PATEL AND KASHMIR

Now that the abrogation of Article 370 is a settled thing, it would perhaps be appropriate to reveal how Kashmir came to India and did not go to Pakistan. The version of what happened step-by-step between Maharaja Hari Singh, the then princely ruler of the state of Jammu & Kashmir, and the then Indian leadership is largely known. It is however, prejudiced to some extent as attempts have been made to give all credit to Jawaharlal Nehru and keep Sardar Vallabhbhai Patel out, so that Patel does not walk away with all the credit for integrating the princely states; to promote the claim that Nehru too played a prominent role in India acquiring Kashmir.

The distinguished historian and columnist Patrick French in his book *Liberty or Death* has revealed what commonsense applied to the limitations of the 1940s could have made possible. Maharaja Hari Singh, the then ruler of Jammu & Kashmir was generally considered a progressive ruler, though the scope of his political reforms was limited.

Patrick French writes that during the weeks leading up to independence, India's last Viceroy Mountbatten had tried to persuade the Maharaja to decide about Kashmir's future, which the latter refused to discuss seriously. Ostensibly, the Maharaja's deferment of a decision on what to do after the British had left stemmed from his firm conviction—voiced to his son yuvraj Dr. Karan Singh as late as July 1947—that the British were never really going to leave India.

Events however, overtook the Maharaja and his state. Come August 15th, 1947 and Hari Singh faced a hostile dispensation. The leader of the pro-Congress All-Jammu and Kashmir National Conference, Sheikh Abdullah had close links with Nehru, whose hostility towards Hari Singh was no secret. A revolt had begun in the southwest of the state in Poonch, which had always historically been antagonistic towards the Maharaja's rule. Muslim farm-workers in Poonch rose against their Dogra landlords, killing some of the local Hindu population and driving others from their homes. This was the beginning of post-independence anti-Hindu violence in J&K. Maharaja Hari Singh slowly began to incline towards India. He realized that his state would be destroyed if he joined Pakistan.

By mid-October 1947, Kashmir had been thrown into a serious crisis. The uprising in Poonch was joined by Pakistani armed brigands, with official encouragement from the Pakistani regime. However, it now comes to light that India wasn't oblivious of the looming threat. For several weeks, Delhi had been secretly supplying weapons and ammunition to the state's armed forces, and making preparations for a military advance.

The tipping point came with the armed invasion of several thousand Pathan tribesmen. On 22nd October, accompanied by a few hundred Poonchis, a rag-tag army began to proceed towards Srinagar. The Pathan raiders were acting on Pakistan's direct orders, though Pakistan denied any complicity in it. On reaching Baramula, Uri, Pattan and Muzaffarabad, the raiders murdered, raped and looted anybody and anything they could lay their hands on. British nuns of Franciscan convent at Baramula too were not spared.

While Hari Singh's royal dynasty despaired of having lost Kashmir, India would not. The government of newly independent India set about recovering the territory. Mountbatten reportedly was convinced of the righteousness of

India's case. He told Patel that he had heard from a British officer, who had heard from another British officer, that the invading Pathans were "very definitely organized". A fortnight later, Mountbatten wrote to King George VI: "It was unquestionable that, if Srinagar was to be saved from pillage by the invading tribesmen, and if the couple of hundred British residents in Kashmir were not to be massacred, Indian troops would have to do the job . . . I therefore made it my business to override all the difficulties which the Commanders-in- Chief, in the course of their duty, raised to the proposal". Thus, the indispensability of India's role in saving Kashmir was acknowledged at the outset.

But a military thrust into a territory which in those days was accessible only with difficulty required weeks, and possibly months of planning. It was only sometime later that Viceroy Mountbatten realized the extent of preparations that must have been made by India, the credit for which goes to Patel. It appears Patel had kept Nehru in the dark about procedural details.

An Indian Army officer present at a meeting of the Defence Committee in New Delhi later that day said Nehru still had doubts about intervention, and "talked about the United Nations, Russia, Africa, God almighty, everybody, until Sardar Patel lost his temper. He said, 'Jawaharlal, do you want Kashmir, or do you want to give it away?' Nehru said, 'Of course I want Kashmir'... and before he could say anything, Sardar Patel turned to me and said, "You have got your orders".

The Indian army drove out the Pakistani Pathan raiders, chasing them all the way to Mirpur. India was militarily well-positioned to recapture the entire state, but Nehru, concerned more about his image internationally, erred grievously in taking the matter to the United Nations, which imposed a stalemate that plagued India for seven decades. With Article 370 having been laid to rest by the Modi administration, it is time to recognize Patel's role in saving Kashmir for India.

* * *

59. WORSHIP COMPLEX AT MEHRAULI

The recent days, it has been repeatedly reported in the media that someone in a position of authority has been intending to remove the two Ganesh idols that adorn the outer walls of what has been forcibly called the "Quwwat-ul-Islam" masjid, next to the Qutb Minar. The Archaeological Survey of India (ASI) during the British days, had installed a tablet at the entrance of this fake mosque, declaring that it was constructed from the rubble of the partly demolished 27 Jain temples.

Reporting on the edifice in 1871, J.D. Beglar, a senior officer of the ASI had recorded that the unsightly layer of irregular stones that covered up the courtyard be removed; it would then be possible to state whether or not a central grand temple existed earlier at the place. The legendary Ibn Battuta was categorical about the mosque being a conversion from a cluster of temples. On the site of the mosque, he wrote, there was a *butkhana* or a house of idols. After the conquest of Delhi, it was turned into a mosque. Even today one cannot fail to notice the images of Ganesh over the plinth of the mosque. Idols of Lord Ganesh (deity) are even today visible on the plinth of the temple in spite of the massive destruction having take place centuries ago. The desecration at Mehrauli was probably the first perpetrated by Muhammad Ghauri. It is situated next to the well-known Qutb Minar. The mosque was located at the citadel which was known as Qila Rai Pithora. The conversion began soon after the second Battle of Tarain, in 1192 AD, wherein Muhammad Ghauri defeated but killed Prithviraj

Chauhan. It might be recalled that in the first Battle of Tarain, it was Prithviraj who had defeated Ghauri and did not kill him, but let him go scot-free. *Kshama veerasya bhushanam* or forgiveness behaves a hero is what the then ruler of Delhi must have had in mind. Let us quote the version given in the Oxford History of Islam: the immense congregational mosque in Delhi known as Quwwat al-Islam (might of Islam) was one of the first concocted in India. Begun in 1192, the mosque stands on the site of pre-Islamic temples whose ruins were incorporated in the structure. The tall iron pillar in the courtyard, originally dedicated to Lord Vishnu around 400 A.D, was re-erected as a trophy to symbolize Islam's triumph over Hinduism.

While many thousand temples are known to have been demolished, there is clear evidence of their having been originally temples. The proof is given either by epigraphs on the structures, or by chroniclers of the Islamic rulers. The intricate carvings and more so, the two Ganesh statuettes on the outer walls are invaluable in this context of history and identification.

Whoever initiated this suit to remove the Ganesh idols from the Qutb complex did so with on obvious mal-intent to obliterate the decisive proof that the Quwwat-al-Islam masjid was the inaugural fake monument of the establishment of sultanate rule in Delhi. However, it is highly fortunate that a Delhi Court has ruled against the removal of the Ganesh idols from the Qutb complex. The additional district court has directed the ASI not to remove the two idols of Lord Ganesh from the Qutb complex till further instructions.

Had the Ganesh idols been removed from the complex, it would have been tantamount to civilizational renunciation of an important part of our heritage and silent acquiescence of Hindu humiliation. Worse, it would also have meant squandering an invaluable evidence, without which any future endeavour of archeological and civilizational revival would be rendered an uphill task.

The Quwwat-ul mosque was converted from 27 Hindu and Jain temples that were destroyed. It is a monument to a people's humiliation. If it were not so, all the statuettes that still adorn the pillars in the mosque need not have been so blatantly displayed. Even after 800 years, they are, as it were, alive for the conquered to see. However, when one reads what Sir Syed Ahmed Khan of Aligarh fame proudly wrote about the destruction of 27 temples, one's impression of Ahmed and his mindset gets shaken. What he wrote is best read in his original words, (from his Urdu book, Asar-us-sanadid, translated by Prof. Khaleeq Anjum, Delhi in 1990, volume I):

Quwwatal-Islam Masjid'd Din Sam alias Shihabu'd-Din Ghauri, conquered Delhi in AH 587 corresponding to AD 1191 corresponding to 1248 Bikarmi, this idol-house (of Rai Pithora) was converted into a mosque. The idol was taken out of the temple, some of the images sculptured on walls or doors or pillars were effaced completely, some were defaced. But the structure of the idol-house kept standing as before. Material from twenty-seven temples, which were worth five crore and forty lakh of Dilwals, were used in the mosque, and an inscription giving the date of conquest and his own name was installed on the eastem gate.

The relish, with which the founder of Aligarh University has written this, is indeed surprising. At that time, the capital of India was still in Calcutta. Had it been transferred to Delhi, his pleasure might perhaps have been greater. For, the Raisina Hill from where India is governed, is only a few miles from Mehrauli where this monument to Hindu humiliation still stands.

* * *

60. SRI LANKAN OPPOSITION WANTS PARLIAMENTARY, NOT PRESIDENTIAL SYSTEM

Press Trust of India has reported that the opposition party of Sri Lanka led by Sajith Premadasa has handed over to the Speaker his proposal to amend the constitution. The desire of Premadasa's party is to scrap the current presidential form of government and replace with it with a system that reinforces what he calls constitutional democracy. Presumably, he means a parliamentary system like the one we have in New Delhi. Premadasa's party ascribes the cause of the current acute economic crisis to an insufficient control of the members of parliament over President Gotabaya Rajapaksa. The implication is that the President has too many free wings whereby he had a free flight and Sri Lanka's economy crashed.

The U.S.A. is the first constitution which was truly presidential and based on, at that time, the theory of the separation of powers. The three powers were legislative, executive and judicial. The working of the British Parliament was critically observed by the creators of the U.S.A. constitution of 1781, on the morrow of the American War of Independence being won by General George Washington in 1776. Distinguished constitutionalists like Alexander Hamilton, James Madison and others found that the British worked their governance well but it was by their faithful character and not with the help of a written down document. Such a written effort was essential because the distances in the United States were considerable and the means of communication were limited. The fastest in the eighteenth century was the horse-back.

The oddities, as practiced in Westminster by the unwritten constitution, were quite a few. The members elected to Parliament were for making laws but soon after their election, they set about forming the government which then depended on parliamentary support. Law making took a back-seat. The upper house, namely the House of Lords helped to form the Privy Council which was the highest law court and therefore the highest level of judiciary where a suit could be appealed to. It was also India's apex court until Independence. Here we have seen the lower house of legislation playing a major role of the legislation providing the apex court of judiciary. We in India practice what we have borrowed from Westminster.

There is no doubt however that the U.S. constitution has helped to provide an excellent system of governance. It has given minimum government with the country achieving a fabulous record of development. In the course of these two and a half centuries or less, the American constitution has been amended only 26 times. We in India have amended our national document some 140 times and have implemented at least a hundred of the amendments. The less one amends, the message is that the constitution is suiting the needs of the country. The more the amendments, it means the less its suitability.

Has Premadasa's party in Colombo thought through the country's problems or are they merely reacting to a crisis, economic as well as ethical. Have the country's rulers been sincere to the performance of their duties? Or have they been frivolous? The experience of many a small nation has been they begin their association with China by buying out the leaders of the junior partner. Thereafter, the Yellow Giant imposes conditions; there is a restaurant in Nairobi, I have been reliably told, wherein Kenyans are not allowed to enter. Mao Zedong used to say that power grows out of the barrel of a gun. Its more modern version is authority flows from the pocket of the master. No constitution can be a solution of such a problem.

Sri Lanka has been unfortunate in having to undergo a series of crises. To name a few, the Easter terrorism, the Covid, both of which are bitter enemies of tourism which has been well developed and was a prolific earner of foreign exchange. Before this was the prolonged and violent civil war near Jaffna. A self-imposed disaster was an attempt at crises development when the economy was under such economic pressure due to the crises. Excellent highways were built as were ports were upgraded; all caused lavish expenditure and the borrowing of money. Then recently followed the Russo-Ukraine war and all its consequences especially the gallops in petroleum prices. For a small country in a weak condition these blows were difficult to withstand.

But It is interesting to note that China increased its footprint significantly during 2010-14, even when a huge amount of developmental assistance came to Sri Lanka from India, a large portion of which were in the form of grants not loans. The affinity of the then Rajapaksa administration towards China for readily extending financial loans to fulfil Mahinda Rajapaksa's developmental vision for the country without questioning the human rights records or progress of the political reconciliation in the post-war period had helped China strengthen its strategic presence in Sri Lanka.

Regardless of these misfortunes as well as mistakes, how would a constitutional metamorphosis help to cure these economic problems. Only money can local as foreign. If anything, what should help is a financial break on the executive, say the President, and not write a new national document when the economic is in hospital.

* * *

61. AN AIRCRAFT REPAIRING A CAR

Through my years in political life, I had never expected an experienced, successful car being repaired, if not also renovated by an aircraft. No doubt, the plane has landed and flown again from many an airport. Being a passenger plane, its function is to fly from one place to another; no matter whether all passengers were comfortable and satisfied or not. Nevertheless, it is the more profitable political aero service today. It has passengers waiting for it at every airport. No sooner than one lot disembarks, another lot fills up the empty seats. Recently the plane landed at Hyderabad but it was not allowed to leave. It booked by locals. To reach Delhi, the owner had to hire another aeroplane. This is also a political wonder of Indian politics.

I wonder why? Is this phenomenon a reflection on the immaturity of India's political class? There has been corruption; there have been a number of dynasties who favour their progeny, thus keep down the other members. There has been casteist biases and what not, but there has also been a full 70 years of constant experience. It seems there are as many elections, state and centre, as there are cricket tournaments. The politicians therefore cannot complain of lack of practice; if anything, there should be a grouse of over exposure. It is true, that Indian political players do not have the long pedigree of their English counterparts who faced their first encounter in the reign of King John soon after 1215 A.D. Most democracies are much newer; some Western democracies, like Germany, Italy, Austria, etc., effectively came into being only after the Second World War.

India's first and then the largest political automobile returned to power at the centre as well as most of the states again and again four times. Its workers and cadres knew all the rules and procedures. Many of them had been authored by them and their superiors.

They certainly had handled election campaigning long before the officers of the Election Commission were probably born. An outstanding problem in those early days was booth capturing. The leading caste of a particular village would surround the booth and then not allow the undesired voters to come anywhere near the captured booth. Instead, the dominant caste members would stamp all the ballot papers inside that booth. For years, no one knew how to tackle this problem. It is the job of the police to maintain law and order. When they failed to control a situation like these, the Central Reserve Police would be pressed into service. When they proved insufficient in numbers, the days of polling began being split into several. In Uttar Pradesh in this year's recently concluded assembly elections in March, the state voted seven times by dividing it into seven sections.

The advent of the laptop, information technology and increasing use of both map political arithmetic in terms of caste presence in various constituencies has driven political parties to court professional statisticians and IT professionals who would chart out and accurately estimate the caste, gender, religions and age divide. This analysis helps parties to select an appropriate candidate. A recent development has been the Shia and Sunni divide. The reason was the developing animosity between these sections, particularly in Pakistan. As the issue of instant triple talaq issue gathered steam, the focus turned to Sunni women because they tended to shift preference away from supposedly secular parties. I am sure experienced politicians must be further refining their figures.

But what of it? The older political parties have considerable talent. The Congress used to be a treasure house of the country's best abilities and knowledge. Until 30 years ago, one could still see trains of youngsters joining the Congress. Broadly speaking, only the ideologically committed people went elsewhere, whether left or right.

Even today, talent should not a problem for any of the large and established parties. What does afflict members is either lack of patience to continue, greed or lack of opportunities to satisfy it. The average party does not coach its young members on what politics is and the career in pursuit of it. This vacuum hit me early in my career when the young workers came to my house. They would ask me: when you are already well off why are wasting your time and energy on what we are doing? Quite a few also wanted to know why I was wasting not only time and energy but also self-respect? This meant that many youngsters join a political party in the hope of enriching themselves as in a business.

Whenever I have spoken to young political workers, I have made it clear that anyone who expects to get rich should kindly give up the vocation. Perhaps, when one gets into a position of power, one might have a chance of enriching oneself. But for how long? Apart from its ethical doubts, the uncertainty and inconsistency of income would constantly stalk the seeker; there are all these question marks. If parties can clarify these simple factors, some of the recruits would ease off; if they do stick around, they would have a greater chance of rising to be upright politicians. Ambition and intrigue are factors that are likely to survive despite all coaching. Then the ethics of parties would be set by the senior leaders. But few leaders have the boldness to bell this cat.

* * *

62. THE JUDICIARY'S ANGST

At the CM-CJs (chief ministers-chief justices) conference held in Delhi on April 30th in Delhi, the Prime Minister and Chief Justice of India were also present. There was a free and frank discussion on why litigation in most of the country's courts was badly languishing; therefore, one could say that justice delayed was justice denied. The Prime Minister said that three and a half lakh undertrials are languishing in prisons and expediting their trials is essential to dispose of as many cases as possible. Most of these undertrials are poor and deprived and deserve early justice. If one solution is to use local languages up to the district level in dispensing judgments, the PM's advice is do so.

Chief Justice Ramanna of the Supreme Court opined that one of the causes for cases piling up has been the non-performance of the legislature and the executive, by itself a contentious issue. The Chief Justice's contention perhaps is that laws passed are after not clearly drafted and lead to unnecessary controversy. Similarly, indifferent administration at the lower levels compel citizens to go to court. The judiciary's perpetual grouse is that there are vacancies in the posts of judges that are not filled promptly enough. There are a number of points that trouble all the three wings of government. What does not great thrown up in that quite a few problems are of a managerial nature and not necessarily of a systemic quality.

It bears iteration here that seventy percent of the cases of litigation arise from the administrative side or the government.

The first step should be to restrain the functionaries from giving adverse decisions unless they are necessary. They must avoid decisions that are issued because they have doubt. The working principle should be to decide in an adversarial way only when certain and not when in doubt; in such cases, doubts should be cleared with the department lawyers or even with the law department; the courts must not make the citizens spend time and money on litigation unless absolutely necessary.

The Prime Minister informed the attendees of the conference of April 30 that the Centre has already repealed 1,450 laws because they had become obsolete. Another 350 laws are already in line to be abrogated. The states should also pursue this line of spring cleaning. Moreover, the drafting of petitions, affidavits as well judgments in the district courts as well as High Courts is tortuous when it comes to terminology. An institution under my charge a few years ago received a judgment that began with Rabindra Nath Tagore and went on in that poetic tone; it was a pleasure to read it. But we had to appeal to the apex court, which turned down the poetic piece. All this means a consumption of time, money and the need for more solicitors, advocates and judges.

Way back in 1976 we had to take legal opinions on a company based in the U.K. The London lawyer produced a draft the next day that was just a little longer than one page. The one that came from India was some ten times as long; the difference was in the style of writing. The advocate in the U.K. preferred the shorter one and rightly so because the points covered were about the same. The other area of editing is appeals; I am not a lawyer, yet have come across a case of tenant eviction which began in Mumbai's Small Causes Court and ended up in Supreme Court! The right to appeal should be reduced to two. Before commencing the final hearing of a matter the judge should decide how much maximum time the two opposing advocates would be permitted. If either advocate exceeds his limit, he should have to pay a stipulated sum of rupees per extra minute, as is done in a taxi for every hundred metres exceeding the minimum fare. Very recently, I heard of an advocate arguing in the apex court for two full working days. Adjournments should cost expensively to the requesting side; say, half the court fee charged to the litigant. Otherwise, adjournments would continue to be availed of freely and popular advocates would carry on getting more and more briefs. Whereas if the client has to pay an adjournment fee, he/she would choose an advocate who has served or money matters in Delhi as well as in other cities.

Judicial activism should be kept to the minimum as also Public Interest Litigation (PILs). The latter was introduced to help the poor and the voiceless to articulate their grievances. It was never meant for the rich and influential to misuse for their purposes, nor for professional lawyers as is often done lately. How to 'plead promptly without failing to communicate with the judge' is one subject that should be taught seriously. In my college days, a great many topics were dealt with. Often, as a result, if an advocate argued speedily, the judges could not always understand the finer edges of the argument. Or else the advocate had to go on pleading indefinitely until he felt he had got his point across, or the judge stopped him from going on. Given the current state of our judicial system, this must be consigned to history.

* * *

63. THE SRI LANKAN CHAOS

Now that a responsible and experienced replacement for the unpopular and forcibly ousted Prime Minister Mahinda Rajapaksa has been appointed, it is time for Sri Lanka to decide how it wants to recoup the current economic depression. On the television, Ranil Wickremesinghe, the new Prime Minister stated that he has a plan for revival. He has some credibility because of his track record, as well as his having served as prime minister five times. What role India wishes to play is for South Block to decide; I personally do feel that India should try and play a significant role in Sri Lanka's revival, especially because of its geopolitical situation. Both New Delhi and Colombo are aware that India has a coastline in the Indian Ocean of over 7,500 kilometres. On the other hand, Sri Lanka is strategically at the southern end of the Indian *praydeep* (peninsula).

Coming to the current situation in our southern island neighbour, there is an unalienable law and order scenario with Sri Lanka's citizens in open conflict with the country's security forces. I have visited Sri Lanka four times in my lifetime and somewhat familiar with the political and ethnic issues there, but I must admit that the torching of the recently deposed Prime Minister Mahinda Rajapaksa's ancestral home in Hambantota by a violent mob has come a bit of a shock to me, as the people there are generally an amiable and easy-going lot. However, keeping cordiality is difficult when one has to wage a daily struggle merely to survive; in Sri Lanka's case, the country has been suffering prolonged power cuts (up to 8 hours a day in several parts of the country, according to several reports), lack of food, and inflated costs of all essential items. Most international agencies have severely downgraded the country's sovereign ratings and its foreign exchange has fallen to Sri Lanka, even in happier times lived mainly on tea, rubber, coconut and tourism as the main earners of revenue for its economy. Moreover, the ruling Rajapaksha dynasty's profligate ways and allegations of corruption against the family have only served to light a torch to an already explosive situation. The discovery of a fleet of some of the world's most expensive automobiles, including Ferraris and Lamborghinis, hasn't exactly been a positive advertisement for responsible behaviour, let alone good governance.

If one talks to a Sinhala scholar or journalist, he may well begin by blaming the cost of Lanka's civil war with its Tamils. He would not admit that the Tamils have been in eastern Sri Lanka since the beginning of civilization. I first visited the country in 1964, and could soon thereafter sense that the Sinhala jealousy towards the Tamils was noticeably intense. For an example, my father-in-law predicted that the next chief executive of the British Ceylon Corporation (like the British Indian Corporation at Kanpur) would be Pereira and not Swamidasan, who was more competent. The former was a Sinhala. The latter subsequently migrated to Australia. This les than even the tip of the iceberg.

The other bias that the majority Sinhalas have harboured has been towards the Hindus. Indians, therefore, would be well-advised to generally field a north Indian and certainly avoid a Tamil or even a Malayali when it comes to official dealing with Lanka. Some thinking Sinhalas apprehend that it is not ruled out that sooner or later, Tamil Nadu could pressurize New Delhi to act against Sinhala interests.

The dark clouds hovering over Sri Lanka were visible as early as 2020, when the global pandemic Covid-19 struck. International rating agencies like Standards & Poor (S&P) and later Moody's downgraded Sri Lanka's long-term sovereign credit ratings. These global agencies had raised the issue of the Sri Lankan government's fiscal health and its ability to service the debt it had incurred from the world Bank and International Monetary Fund (IMF). The war over Ukraine has further worsened things for the island nation.

The crisis in the Emerald Isle needs urgent succor and India must decide how far it wants to go in order to help. For the record, the new Prime Minister has already voiced his government's priority of furthering relations with India. Secondly, Colombo must persuade its present creditors to wait patiently, so that what India sends would be of help to Lanka's future rather than applying balm to its past. India could then offer that proportion of Sri Lanka's future needs which the island country can earn and utilize to pay back.

We have mentioned about the mutual stake in the Indian Ocean. Both countries must protect each other's interest in this vast pond. This ought to include a Sri Lanka administration being more sympathetic to the people of Jaffna.

Any Indian loan(s) should ideally be for use to procure all or any goods/items from India. We are capable of supplying anything from butter to guns. The Sinhalas are a frank, friendly and pleasure-loving people and not very money-conscious. As was revealed by a scholar in Kolkata, while Karl Marx had said that "religion is the opium of the masses" a loan is the opium of the classes. It is in this innocent sprit the Sri Lankas have borrowed money. Any new lender should be conscious of this.

* * *

64. RAPE AND MARITAL RAPE

When there was no institution of marriage, the question of marital rape did not arise. Marriages were introduced to legitimize the children and give them a social identity. With the advent of Christianity, marriages began being monogamous which lent more dignity to the wife in her marriage as well as society. It perhaps introduced also the possibility of unweaponized rape because it left the husband no alternative spouse. Although rape implies not only force but also illegitimacy whereas in the compound of matrimony this latter factor does not exist. The spouses may quarrel over what they prefer when and eventually agree to disagree. But to escalate the difference of opinion to the heights of rape which would lead the one or the other spouse to the police, is to inaugurate a divorce. It may be done, but why dramatize a difference of desire in bed into a crime called rape?

An allegation of rape by the husband of rape would be the beginning of the end of the marriage. What is the purpose of the proposed new device? Such a union would, in any case, break up. Rape in marriage being sanctified by law is a nihilistic thought, a philosophical endeavour to break up, if not also destroy society. After World War II, Europe has been experimenting with 'living together' without matrimony. The single parent children are often unfortunate in the matter of discipline as well as a focus in life. The parent, in keeping peace with the child, tends to spoil her/him. Why should we disrupt our society? Surely, we do not wish to decline as Europe is doing.

The term "marital rape" is ambiguous, if not misleading. It is used to describe sexual acts committed without and/or against her will by the woman's husband. He may use physical force, the threat of force either against her or another individual related to her or whose safety and well-being she fears for, or implied harm based on prior assaults, causing the woman to fear that physical force will be used against her, or some harm may befall her or those who may be close/dear to her, if she resists.

It is also important to note that the misuse of sex within relationships is not confine itself to males or females. Both men and women can learn to use this basic human instinct to create greater intimacy and, conversely, both sexes can learn to use sex as a weapon within a marriage. Married couples who utilize sexuality for power and control will soon learn that the marriage suffers in many areas. In general, open communication is often diminished, conflicts tend to arise readily, and arguments often remain unresolved. Unhealthy passive-aggressive or openly aggressive behaviour often becomes the norm.

If equality is any consideration for resorting to marital rape as crime, there is seldom a question of equal partners. Whichever is more intelligent and grows further with time dominates in every marriage. In my experience, it is the wife, in India, who manipulates the husband more often than the husband dictating to him. When it comes to the bedroom, one must remember that the male and female systems are differently motivated. Moreover, if the husband can rape, the wife can seduce for which it may be difficult to find evidence or proof and therefore a punishment.

Marriage is not exactly like a business partnership. It is a multi-faceted combination which grows as well as changes as well as evolves with time or age. The fear of criminal punishment would knock this joy out of the friendship which is what an ideal marriage is. Christianity defines it as a oneness, divine and indivisible. The Hindu matrimony is and was also a sacrament, and after the passing of the Hindu Code Bill in 1955 also became a monogamy. Such institutions led a great deal of security, reassurance, care and love unless the spouses cannot get on. The chances of getting on so much higher when the spirit of the union is sacramental. There is reportedly so much fear of loneliness that Mother Teresa was awarded the Novel Prize for promoting Missionaries of Charity in Calcutta in 1979. In this much faster moving world why do we went to introduce greater scope of crime and punishment for marital rape?

Further, the issue, or allegation of marital rape may not remain confined to physical violation of a woman's body alone. It is not inconceivable that tomorrow, allegations against the husband not giving his wife money, or 'enough' of it, might be included in its ambit. A wife who alleges abuse might not want a divorce as she needs a roof over her head. Criminalizing marital relations will not help her in any way.

Over the years, I have come across more happy marriages than unhappy ones. In the middle classes certainly so, lower down the scale, a little of this phenomenon, mostly due to the husband's surrender to the bottle. Such a society, in any case, does not deserve to be distributed or even threatened. The law on marital rape as a crime certainly encourages both. On the flip side, what would be the benefit of the law penetrating potentially every bedroom in the country?

* * *